# Praise for *A New Kind of Party Animal*

"[Mitchell] makes useful points: that older people have always belittled the political interests and commitment of the young, that there is a far stronger political community within Generation X than is generally acknowledged and—this is perhaps most important—that rather than automatically allying themselves with the major parties, the young are 'hesitant to embrace a single ideology' and often describe themselves as 'independent.'"

—Jonathan Yardley, *The Washington Post*

"[Mitchell] is a gifted writer, and her descriptions often shimmer."
—Natasha Stovall, *The Village Voice*

"*A New Kind of Party Animal* is an intelligent, even inspirational, opening salvo in what could result in further discussions of the many true and diverse states of young political minds and where they will lead us in the next century. *A New Kind of Party Animal* goes to the heart of common misconceptions, proving that 18–35s do vote and do get involved."

—Jennifer Nix, *On the Issues*

"This is an important read for anyone who wants to lead in the twenty-first century. Goethe once said: 'knowing is not enough; we must apply. Willing is not enough; we must do.' This generation—my children's generation—is learning, applying, and doing. They are our nation's future and cannot and should not be ignored."

—Senator Bob Kerrey

"If you believe that young Americans are disengaged from public service, Michele Mitchell will prove you wrong. Her feisty book is a splendid addition to the political debate, illustrating that her generation is, indeed, revitalizing our dismal politics."

—Tanya Melich, author of *The Republican War Against Women*

"On just about every page, Michele Mitchell deftly punctures another stereotype about her generation. Political operatives, the press, and the public will learn a lot in these pages about the attitudes and motivation of the young men and women who will shape the first part of the twenty-first century in America."

—Tom Brazaitis, Washington Bureau Chief,
*The Plain Dealer* (Cleveland) and coauthor
of *War without Bloodshed: The Art of Politics*

"Brisk and colorful prose . . . [Mitchell] faithfully records the activities of young people across the ideological spectrum."

—Louis Jacobson, *The Plain Dealer* (Cleveland)

"Mitchell's book may inspire a younger reader to change the world."

— *Kirkus*

"[Mitchell] offers a point that's well worth making. . . . Highly readable."

—Mary Lynn F. Jones, *The Hill*

"Michele Mitchell convincingly destroys the myth that today's young people are destroying the country's future. [Her] book is a comfort to young people who think their generation is misunderstood and a delight for anyone frustrated with today's politics."

—Melissa Suarez, *Greensboro News & Record*

"Mitchell offers a welcome portrait of a generation bent on righting societal ills through their own brand of homespun politics. [She] unearths a heaping amount of compelling data to back up her numerous anecdotes, which serves to keep the pages turning at a good clip."

— *Thirty Days Books*

"Michele Mitchell bucks the prevailing media clichés and takes a view much more in line with reality."

—David Bailey, *Sky*

"Clever . . . This book debunks stereotypes about twenty- and thirty-somethings."

—Paul West, *The Olympian*

"The perspective of youth sheds a useful light on some of the issues of the day. . . . Maybe by writing angry, optimistic books like hers, we can help capture the magic of being young and pioneering—and somehow make it last."

—Jeff Horwich, *Louisville Courier-Journal*

# A NEW KIND OF PARTY ANIMAL

## How the Young Are Tearing Up
## the American Political Landscape

# Michele Mitchell

*A Touchstone Book*
*Published by Simon & Schuster*

*TOUCHSTONE*
*Rockefeller Center*
*1230 Avenue of the Americas*
*New York, NY 10020*

*Designed by Sam Potts*

*Manufactured in the United States of America*

*1   3   5   7   9   10   8   6   4   2*

*The Library of Congress has catalogued the Simon & Schuster edition as follows:*
*Mitchell, Michele.*
*A new kind of party animal : how the young are tearing up the American political landscape /*
*Michele Mitchell.*
*p.        cm.*
*Includes bibliographical references and index.*
*1. Young adults—United States—Political activity.*
*1. Title.*
*HQ799.7.M57      1998*
*305.235'0973—dc21      98-10495 CIP*

*ISBN 0-684-83697-1*
*0-684-85441-4 (Pbk)*

*For my parents, who always knew*

# Contents

# *Acknowledgments*

Sarah Baker and Lydia Wills guided me.

Eric Anderson, Tom Brazaitis, Mary Cummings, Sean Dougherty, Jim Duffy, Eric Federing, Jeff Frank, Walt Harrington, George Knue, Randall Lane, Adrian MacGillivray, Dan McGirt, Heather McLeod, Craig Neff, Joan Patakas, Howell Raines, Kimberly Schuld, Sue Semegran, Patrick Tuohey, and Ellen Weiss educated me.

Mike Towle and David LaGesse fed me.

Jen Cohen, Jennifer Ross Gaynor, and Jeannie Bonner listened (oh so patiently) to me.

Tim Charters, Sarah Claassen, Jill Nienhiser, and especially Sonya Mitchell put up with me.

Michael Collins, Jan and Dale Goldfarb, Suzanne Hendrickson, and Susan Raines supported me.

Jonathan Ortmans, Tana Rosenblatt, Virginia Martin, and everyone at the Public Forum Institute housed me.

My wonderful sources trusted me.

And, finally, Representative Pete Geren hired and then inspired me.

# Introduction

**SHOCK, HORROR AS PIKE GULPS DOWN RARE BIRD**

*London* (Reuters)—Birdwatchers who had traveled from all over Britain to glimpse a rare, migrating bird watched in horror as a giant fish gobbled it down.

The *Sun* quoted the "twitchers", as birdwatchers are known, as saying the 4-foot pike gulped the red-necked phalarope in one bite. "It was like a scene from 'Jaws'," one said. "One second the bird was swimming—the next there was a snap and a splash and it vanished."

Only a few feathers remained to prove that the exotic waterbird had visited the Leichestershire reservoir.

$B$ob Meagher usually rounded off his day by wandering through the wire stories. This one, he sent to everyone he knew—Capitol Hill, beyond, it didn't matter. Ah, the beauty of E-mail, Bob thought. He snickered and tapped at the top, "Kinda puts the whole thing in perspective, doesn't it?"

He meant the unrelenting rush of "look!-the-new-youth-movement-in-politics!" proclamations belched out by newspapers and television. One more mention of "apathetic" or "cynical" or that damn alphabet letter and Bob thought his brain would explode. Since he figured his friends thought the same way, they would see the parallel. Of course, some had more time for allusion than others. "Why did Bob send us a fish story?" Lynn Marquis asked after she read it.

But Bob had hit it right. Faster than a ten-pound pike could gulp a one-pound bird, all those desperately analytical generational articles were going to end up like the feathers of the red-necked phalarope—the only evidence that the ill-conceived assumptions had even once appeared.

It had happened before. And before, and before. Memory had edited it out by now. But once, the headlines had read: "Our Muddled Youth"; "Youth Gone Loco"; "The Perpetual Youth Problem." Once, journalist Maxine Davis had written in *The Literary Digest*: "Today's younger generation accepts whatever happens to it with sheep-like apathy." And once, *Harper's* magazine had crowed, "A lost generation is even now rotting before our eyes."

The rest of America had dreaded the day when these "confused, disillusioned and disenchanted" young people would grow up and take over the country. But the peers of John Kennedy, Ronald Reagan, and George Bush probably would have argued that they had done a first-rate job, what with winning World War II and all. They might now tenderly regard their past—how many times have Dear Abby and Ann Landers run those columns about an alleged study of the "Top Ten School Problems" in the 1930s (gum chewing, giggling, hair pulling), sanctimoniously comparing this to the "Top Ten School Problems" of today (drugs, violence, promiscuity)? Too bad it isn't true. Such a study never existed. No matter how thick the lenses are on those rose-colored glasses, the generation that fought World War II was never initially hailed as saviors and survivors, all grit and glory. The fact is, none of their elders had expected them to amount to anything much at all.

Thirty years later, the "slack" and the "doomed generation" arrived. This time there were actual polls to record that the strongest impression the then-young Americans made on their World War II–veteran parents was "not much." Jerry Rubin, Abbie Hoffman, and Tom Hayden promptly warned their peers, "Don't trust anyone over thirty." They led the student riots from the muddied and torn grounds of Grant Park to the doors of the 1968 Democratic convention and chanted, "The whole world is watching!" Four years later, Rubin and Hoffman had a publishing contract with Warner, air-conditioned offices at the political conventions, and had long passed that magic age. They amended their statement. Now, they cautioned, "Don't trust anyone over forty." Meanwhile, apathy creeped on to college campuses. In 1971, the Dartmouth valedictorian proclaimed, "I have made no plans because I have found no plans worth making." And on the West Coast, the Berkeley *Daily Californian* noted, "All too many people are just waiting for life rather than living." Such misgivings have gone the way of the polyester leisure suit, now that this group dominates the media. They don't remember it. More typical is the fond reflection of *The Washington Post:* "Student rallies, speeches and petitions flooded almost every campus." Then, added the paper on a more sour note, "Today, hardly a whimper."

It is a lament as old as the country itself—"Kids today!" eyes rolling heavenward, a slight shake of the head as the words hiss into sympathetic ears. Even when patriot recruits, most just barely out of their teens, marched through the streets of New York in 1776, shouting, "The rising world shall sing of us a thousand years to come/And tell our children's children the wonders we have done," no doubt their parents pressed thin hands to wan faces and sighed, "Kids today!" At the 1996 Democratic convention, a forty-five-year old press director was appalled when blank stares greeted his nostalgic rendition of "The Whole World Is Watching!"

"Um," said a reporter who had been all of one year of age in 1968, "is that the new CNN slogan?"

"This just proves the point," the press director said with authority. "Young people today are apathetic, cynical slackers."

Then again, twenty-eight years had passed since the riots, when baby-boom protesters had complained about "the generation gap" between them and their World War II–veteran parents. At that point, it had only been twenty-three years since the end of World War II. Gaps are arbitrary. Time rolls on.

So of course it would be *Time* magazine that ran one of the first generational profiles of us. It was the summer of 1990. I flipped through the slick pages and learned that "the twentysomething generation is balking at work, marriage and baby-boomer values. Why are today's young adults so skeptical?" Gee, that wasn't condescending or anything. I was barely twenty. I attended school full-time and worked part-time. That couldn't exactly be called "balking." And as for marriage, well, I was *twenty*. Baby-boomer values? According to *Time*, "the 1960s brought everything embodied in the Summer of Love." I assumed that meant drugs and promiscuity, the two things most often mentioned in sixties retrospectives. But even those weren't exclusive to the boomers. Today's senior citizens smoked enough marijuana in their youth to warrant cries of a "drug crisis" and the making of *Reefer Madness*. They also had enough premarital sex to prompt sociologists to predict that "virginity at marriage would be extinct for men by 1950 and for women by 1965."

But, sticking with its theme, *Time* magazine went even further. My peers "don't even seem to know how to dress," according to sociologist Paul Hirsch. *Time* then concluded that we "so far are . . . hardly recognized as anything at all." It did give us one nod—that we were "freshly minted grown-ups"—but that only made me wonder: Where, exactly, did *Time* get off, judging any of us at this point in life? The magazine was just like the twitchers on the shore of the Leichestershire reservoir. It clutched at a few feathers as if those represented the presence of something whole.

Of course, the article was just the beginning. Two years later, after graduating from college and landing my first job—as a press secretary on Capitol Hill—I fairly choked on all the articles, analyses, and editorials, and Bob Meagher was sending out a steady stream of E-mail commentary about it. None of us should have been too surprised. We weren't the first to be dissected in an attempt to figure out what we would do with the country when we took over. And the stakes got higher with the realization that we—the ones born between 1961 and 1981—would be the largest potential voting-age bloc by 1998 (we outnumber the "boom"—born between 1943 and 1960—by ten million).[1] Despite all the profiles, interviews, news clips, and sound bites, we haven't been unraveled. The media, in a hurry more than ever because of the rapidity of technology, started in on us too soon. "It's not that the media aren't anxious to give this group air time," wrote *Washington Post* economic reporter Clay Chandler, "it's that they don't know where to point the camera."

Again, like the twitchers, they caught a few glimpses. They saw that we didn't buy into every sales pitch that came our way. Madison Avenue and Hollywood stomped and gnashed in frustration as seemingly "sure things" like the I'm-so-lost-and-life-sucks movie *Reality Bites*, well, bit. This must mean, deduced the media, that young people were cynical. And then there were the ripples from the Great Protests of the '60s—*Time*, not seeing any 18–35s marching with placards, admonished them for taking for granted "many of the real goals of the '60s . . . [like] feminism." So, young people must be apathetic. Most alarming to the media was the

---

[1] In their seminal book, *Generations*, William Strauss and Neil Howe define the "boom" generation as beginning with the 1943 "victory babies," which precedes the demographic "boom" by three years, and ends four years before the demographic "boom" concludes. Most pollsters and even demographers agree; pollster Patrick Caddell notes that those born in the early 1960s "have had different experiences and their attitudes don't really fit with those of the baby boomers."

rapid rate at which so many newspapers and magazines had folded or merged over the past ten years. Journalism schools scurried to redraft curriculums, because, evidently, the printed word was about to become obsolete in the cold face of emerging technologies, and because, the media assumed, young people did not read.

Presumptions like these ground in so deeply that the media couldn't shake them when it finally began to reconsider labels and trends by the mid-1990s. A 1997 *Newsweek* editorial by a twenty-six-year-old senior editor had the headline, "Where Have All the Causes Gone?" and lamented, "All the Big Causes seem to be settled . . . we came in during the falling apart." This smacked of a forty-year-old editor's concept of younger Americans—from the takeoff on Peter, Paul and Mary's "Where Have All the Flowers Gone?" to the sorry-you-missed-the-fun smugness—and had then been assigned to a twenty-six-year-old for cover. The letters that poured in from readers seemed to bear this out. The "boomers" wrote comments like, "As the daughter of a World War II veteran . . . and as the sister of a Vietnam casualty . . . my gut has struggled with this question for years." The actual young Americans wrote back, "We are making our history every day."

Then, *Time* magazine published its version of a mea culpa, stating one moment that "Gen X is committed" and in the next lamenting the end of the days like "1966 . . . when young people still believed they could change the world." The actual young Americans wrote back that "the generation labeled X was a target market all too aware of being targeted"; "Dismissing us as 'do-nothings' gave us plenty of leeway to do everything we wanted while no one was watching"; and "What do you mean we have given up on idealism and given in to the fact that we cannot change the world?"

"It's *happening*," Greg Gillam said, a bit melodramatically, when Jerry Morrison announced that he would challenge one of the original good ol' boys for office in Chicago. As the man who packed beautiful women into the smoky confines of Sweet Alice every Tuesday for an open-mike night, even what seemed to be wild pronouncements by Greg could not be ignored. He was plugged in, but not just to the hip and the now. Greg knew what was grounded and lasting. The twenty-eight-year-old was well aware, just as many of his peers were, that the answer to the irresistible question—*What comes next?*—had already been laid out: chip by chip; fingernails grimy and hands calloused; ballots stacked; issues mapped; glass ceilings shattered. The answer is all there for the 70 million of us born between 1961 and 1980. This is the number who can presently vote. Truly for lack of a better term, we are the 18–35s. Although this generation technically ends with those born in 1981, why pull a *Time* on seventeen-year-olds and saddle them with more assumptions? I hated it when it happened to my peers. Bob Meagher hated it—and so did our Capitol Hill colleagues, Lynn Marquis and Robert George. In Chicago, Jerry Morrison, Roger Romanelli, and Greg Gillam would rather have knocked back several glasses of lighter fluid than acknowledge it. In Durham, Quillie Coath Jr. and Charles McKinney scoffed at it. In Sacramento, Kim Alexander first dashed off chastising letters to reporters and public figures before deciding that action was the best revenge.

Most of us didn't know each other beyond our state lines. Aside from my meeting Greg Gillam at Northwestern University, we all pretty much circled in our own worlds. No wonder—we ranged from foster kids to trust-fund babies; from Tidewater stock to descendants of slaves; East to South to North to West; parents single, divorced, nuclear at best. Still, we were linked. When it came to politics, we said "show me" when offered a promise. We believed in only what we could see with our own eyes. We demanded accountability. We did not unconditionally offer up our loyalty. We had no preconceived notions of gender and leadership as mutually exclusive terms. We connected through technologies that we were creating.

And with our peers, we were changing the political scene. We didn't *mean* to. Most 18–35s professed a deep and heartfelt disdain for anything faintly tinged with the word "political," prompting the director of the youth-oriented group Democrats With Attitude to say, "Politics needs to be made fun for them. . . . Fun events, fun logos, fun things." This meant comedians doing stand-up routines, brightly colored beach balls for rallies, and "Blues Brothers–type sunglasses and cool T-shirts." *The Washington Post* observed, "What young 'post-partisans' forget is that issues inflame passions, and passions drive and sustain participation— through brutal campaigns; long, boring nights of phone banking and canvassing; and years (perhaps decades) in the minority." So 18–35s believed in fun, not issues? They weren't passionate or dedicated? Well, what was it, then, when Quillie Coath and Charles McKinney felt propelled into community activism in the wake of rising juvenile crime rates? All the hysterical statistics and articles, and the diatribes delivered on the floor of the House of Representatives and in the Senate, reduced little bodies of frustrated childhood into pat lines. The children who testified at a congressional hearing in 1996 wept and poured out their terror to a panel of suits who couldn't understand murder outside the war zones they had fought in over fifty years ago.

"How many more kids have got to be killed?" asked a thirteen-year-old girl from Indianapolis who had survived an accidental shooting. "I get scared that if I just look at the wrong person in the wrong way, I might get shot or stabbed."

And another, a fourteen-year-old from Washington State: "I saw Hank lying on the ground. He wasn't dead yet, but he was lying there, twitching. It was a terrible thing, terrible to see someone you know, someone who used to make you laugh, lying there, dying right in front of you."

The anger that swelled up in Quillie and Charles—"How did we get to this point where this kid watches his buddy twitching on the ground?" Charles demanded—was passionate and political. Getting involved in the community could be nothing but political, from the city council meetings to the county hearings that they would have to attend in order to get things done. "If we don't do something," Quillie asked, "who will? The clock is ticking."

Greg Gillam ended up doing his open-mike show because of politics. If anyone potentially fit the stereotypical "slacker" image, it would have been Greg. His first few weeks as a newly minted college graduate and artist-in-making (he didn't even know what kind of art he wanted to do) were spent wrapped in a secondhand fatigue jacket and eating peanut butter three times a day, sometimes straight from the jar. He lived in a studio that had wood paneling that didn't match from sheet to sheet and dingy gold shag carpeting. "Oh my god, Greg," said one of his friends when she saw it, "your apartment looks like a porn movie set." Then, in January, the building's heat went off one night. Chicago is not merely cold that time of year. Colorado is cold. Michigan is cold. Chicago has a wind howling off the ice of Lake Michigan like a banshee out of hell. It bites the eyes until tears protectively spring up and freeze to the lashes. So when the bitterness swept in and there was no heat at all for over a week, Greg sat in his apartment, despondently staring at the wood-paneled walls as his breath came in white puffs. And that was when the hot water went.

Greg called his alderman—or, city councilman—to complain. Only so many baths could be taken by heating up pots on stove burners. And with that phone call, Greg found out that his rat-bastard landlord had stopped paying the utility bills *and* the mortgage. The bank filed a foreclosure action, and the landlord was still skimming whatever rent he could, coming out ahead by not paying the bills. Suddenly Greg found himself organizing a tenants' rights campaign, something he never suspected he had in him. When the bank settled, giving each tenant $1,500 to move out of the building, he decided it was worthwhile to get involved.

He wasn't thinking on a national level. What went on in Washington barely registered, and why should it? Washington didn't bust his landlord. Besides, Greg could *see* the difference locally. Because he checked out the landlord's scam, nearly a hundred people were able to move to better neighborhoods, thanks to the money from the bank. Not only that, but he never would have had the guts to stand up on a stage and read his own poetic ramblings to an audience if he hadn't delved into untried territory, which gave a semi-employed twenty-five-year-old newfound self-confidence. It paid off in 1995 when he got his own show at Sweet Alice. "I could never have handled a bar full of people different from me if I hadn't gotten involved in politics," he said. And then, of course, he might not have heard about Jerry Morrison's campaign.

Jerry sure didn't expect *Chicago* to come up with a new, palatable brand of politics. That would be like saying in the '80s that Mike Ditka, beloved former player and coach of the Bears who even looked like a bear, could ever leave town. Then again, Mike Ditka *did* leave town—albeit in 1997, and things did change. Maybe they stood a chance when they decided to take on the Democratic machine. "We wanted to try something new," Jerry explained. "You know, like *voting*. If anyone's going to take on the establishment, it's going to be us. Imagine running a campaign on high voter turnout—not just targeting a few sure votes. That'd make 'em panic! They won't know what to do."

It wasn't politics, at least in its strictest definition, that prompted Kim Alexander to be one of the first to put a voting issues guide on the Internet. She didn't think her peers were getting the correct—read "unfiltered"—information, and she didn't trust the pundits or the pols to dish it straight. "It's a matter of self-interest," she said, shrugging. "I can't wait around for someone else to do it." But it was politics that made her list late campaign contributions on the Internet. In an election year that would be defined by campaign funding scandals, Kim Alexander threw disclosure wide open with "electronic filing."

And on Capitol Hill, well, it would be difficult to call anything on Capitol Hill *un*political. Even the homeless woman who sat outside the Longworth House Office Building every morning Congress was in session, still protesting the Vietnam War, could be found next to her placards, reading *The Washington Post*. When I was there, Capitol Hill happened to be the most partisan place during the most partisan time since the Taft administration. And especially when jobs literally depended on votes and party loyalty, certainly no staffers had ever broken ranks. But with the young electorate already marked by a lack of party identification (over 60 percent of young people did not identify with either the Democrats or the Republicans), Bob Meagher, Lynn Marquis, Robert George, and other 18–35s who worked on Capitol Hill weren't any different. The young staffers also followed their peers in their lack of gender bias when it came to politics. This unconventional combination left the Washington establishment with the distinctly uncomfortable feeling that a confrontation was coming.

Whether you consider politics a dirty word or not, it is a microcosm of society. If it's happening there, it's going on in other areas, too. The 18–35s didn't confine their independent inclinations to the political arena. Instead of following the previous two generations into large corporations, nearly 10 percent of twenty-five- to thirty-four-year-olds are starting their own businesses, a rate almost three times higher than that of any other age group. They are also less likely to sell out to larger companies. So when twenty-four-year-old Dineh Mohajer came up with Hard Candy nail polish when she needed blue nail polish to go with her blue platform shoes, and when twenty-nine-year-old Wende Zomnir started Urban Decay nail polish (with colors like "Gash" and "Uzi"), and when it became apparent that neither was about to sell their equity, larger cosmetic firms went at them. Revlon, for one, put out polish like "Blood" and "Gun Metal." (Zomnir dismissed this philosophically, saying, "When they start a product they do focus groups and studies. I just put out the colors I dig.")

In Hollywood, the big studios attempted to reach 18–35s with contrived "young" movies like *Reality Bites*. But it was independent efforts by peers like Richard Linklater *(Dazed and Confused)* and Edward Burns *(The Brothers McMullen)* that struck. Then again, Burns's movie dealt with the problems of commitment in relationships. And even there, in the most personal trend of all, Burns touched on a plot that was tailor-made for a generation marrying later than previous ones. None of the 18–35s wondered about this, even if older people did. No other group before had been raised by such a large number of divorced parents. In 1980, only 56 percent of children lived with two once-married parents. Another 14 percent lived with at least one previously married parent, 11 percent with a stepparent, and 19 percent with one parent. Four-fifths of their parents professed to be happier after their divorces. A majority of 18–35s felt otherwise. As a result, marriage became something to be taken very seriously. The average age for marriage today is twenty-seven for men and twenty-five for women—up from twenty-three and twenty-one, respectively, in 1970. Young Americans approached commitment to marriage as cautiously as they did commitment in politics.

But still. . . .

"They don't vote."

"They don't read."

"They don't even seem to know how to dress."

The litany smacks of a Greek chorus desperately in need of Prozac. "For a long time," said Kim Alexander, "I looked to older people for validation of my ideas. I kept waiting for them to understand what it is that I'm doing. Then all of a sudden I realized, *I don't need* their *validation*—I should be validating the ideas of the people coming up behind me, who *do* get what I'm doing." So the young people of the United States go about their political business, thrumming just below the detectable surface, cracking the crust in enough fits and starts to unnerve—and intrigue—the older Americans as they ruminate on their wars, their protests, their music, their politics. And, as their elders had done about them, they wonder what the hell this new crop is going to do with their country.

"Either get it," Kim said, "or get out of the way. We can work around you."

We must consider each generation as a distinct nation, with a right, by the will of its majority, to bind themselves, but none to bind the succeeding generation, more than the inhabitants of another country.

—Thomas Jefferson,
in a letter to John Eppes,
June 24, 1813

## CHAPTER ONE

# PARTY OUT OF BOUNDS

## A STRONG VOTE FOR OUR COMMUNITY

Government works only when people participate. In the past two months alone, Morrison has registered one thousand new voters in the 32nd Ward. As your committeeman, Morrison will register 10,000 voters, hold issue forums, and get people out on election day.

## A NEIGHBORHOOD FOR EVERYBODY

Jerry stared at the slick paper of the handout, his face staring right back at him. He wore a tie and a suit in the photo, something he knew his friends wouldn't let him live down. They were used to seeing him in T-shirts and backward baseball caps. And at the bottom of the paper was "Paid for by Citizens for Morrison." Man, oh man, this was for real. Citizens for Morrison! Jerry had to blink to believe it. Then, he couldn't stop smiling. Push the boundaries. This was as independent as a candidacy got these days in Chicago.

Jerry Morrison was thirty. Jesus, when he was a kid he thought thirty was *old.* His father had three kids by that age. Jerry didn't have any, which was fine by him. He still fell a bit below the eldest of his generation, a dismayingly disengaged group, if press reports were to be believed. Right. Jerry didn't swallow it. The same journalists who made that call were also the ones who declared a half-baked little essay by a youth group named Third Millennium to be the '90s equivalent of the 1962 Port Huron Statement, which had been put out by Tom Hayden's group, Students for a Democratic Society. When the self-declared Original Youth Movement grew up, they saw themselves as entrusted to discover the next one. But what they were looking for, subconsciously or otherwise, was *themselves.* Jerry didn't have time to coax them out of this and along to reality. He had a campaign to run.

Of course, his family was a bit disconcerted that he was doing this on the *north* side of the city. Jerry grew up on the southeast side, where the buildings were brick, solid, not stylish. The people there liked to think of themselves in the same way. The Hawk that cut across Lake Michigan every winter never stopped South Siders from going to Soldier Field. Real men just threw on parkas and took coffee in thermoses. Men from the North Side watched the game on big screen televisions in sports bars, warming their hands on cappuccino. Real men went to Comiskey Park. The North Side pansies went to Wrigley Field. Real men challenged their arteries with Polish sausage. The North Side yuppies coddled theirs with bran muffins.

No Morrison had lived beyond the north-south dividing line of Madison Avenue—and there were a lot of Morrisons, who fell into either steel or politics. Jerry's aunt Carmie over in Calumet City was the one aberration, but only because she combined both of these. She owned the Rose and Crown Tavern in the blue-collar neighborhood just outside the Chicago line. Most of her customers worked in the steel mills, and she held fund-raisers for

A NEW KIND OF PARTY ANIMAL

union candidates. Jerry's father was a tavern regular. Until the strike in '59, Monk Morrison had worked as a boilermaker. The job was hot and dirty, not to mention dangerous. Monk didn't go back when the strike ended. He opened a butcher shop instead and raised a union family in the back of the store.

Jerry hacked frozen slabs of beef alongside him, watching as his father's hands twisted into knots of arthritic bone. After working all day in cold water and forty-degree coolers for twenty years, that happened. But Monk did what he set out to accomplish: send his three kids to college. True to the unwritten barriers in Chicago, Monk had never been to Wrigley Field for a Cubs game. So Jerry caused a minor family scandal when he married his college girlfriend, Larisa, and moved to the Bucktown neighborhood on the North Side. His parents refused to visit for three years. As far as Monk was concerned, his son had gotten "uppity."

Actually, his son was getting mad. Jerry lived in the Thirty-second Ward of Chicago, which cobbled together forty-eight precincts, from Ukrainian Village to Wicker Park to parts of Wrigleyville. Pockets of old Polish neighborhoods mixed with the young ranks, the latter balancing mostly between well-off urbanites and nearly starving artists. Well, there were some not-so-hungry artists. Liz Phair lived there for a while, as did members of the Smashing Pumpkins, Urge Overkill, and Material Issue. Despite these alternative riffs, Terry Gabinski had been the alderman for the Thirty-second Ward for over thirty years.

Gabinski had been handpicked by none other than Dan Rostenkowski, who had been one of the most powerful members of Congress until his defeat and indictment on corruption charges in 1994. As chairman of the Ways and Means Committee, which decided how the national budget should be divvied up, Rostenkowski took his steaks bloody at Morton's and pretty much cut deals the same way. He ended his career in a federal jail, suffering from prostate cancer. His colleagues remembered him fondly,

*Party Out of Bounds*

though. Rostenkowski might have been crooked, but he kept his word.

Rostenkowski and Gabinski both were products of the Democratic machine, and nothing branded Chicago more deeply than the machine's power ("The press seems to have a taste for the word 'machine,'" said former Cook County Democratic chairman Jacob Arvey in 1952, "maybe because the right word—'organization'—is too long to fit in a headline"). "Chicago is like the old Soviet Union," one activist once said. "It's a one-party state. There are just different factions of Democrats." Liberals, moderates, conservatives, anarchists. All the divisions fell under the enormous umbrella of the Democratic Central Committee. Each of the fifty members of the central committee represented wards in the city. They picked candidates for Congress, state legislators, and judgeships, and controlled about 3,000 jobs. Terry Gabinski was the committeeman for the Thirty-second Ward. In Chicago, it wasn't unusual to hold two elected offices at the same time.

The ruling party had certain ways. For one thing, candidates had to be picked to run by the central committee. Ambitious political hopefuls had to be loyal soldiers and play by hierarchical rules. That was a gamble Jerry didn't care to take. Many people had done exactly that and had never been chosen. And then, even if they were tapped, they were always beholden to the machine. That wasn't Jerry's idea of how politics should work. Besides, he thought boundaries were meant to be stretched. As he saw it, either he and his buddies got involved in city politics now and on their own terms or, Jerry told them, "We can allow morons to keep slating idiots."

Jerry knew he could take the brawling, schmoozing political realities of Chicago and put his own stamp on them. He stood stocky and square-jawed, with an open grin and a firm handshake. "I look like a Chicago cop who's seen too many doughnuts," he said. He was grounded in community organizing, from starting block clubs to running the Northwest Side Anti-Gang Task Force. So when he decided he wanted a run at Gabinski, he fully realized what he was signing up for. Just as important, he knew what he wanted to do. He had no intention of being one of those wishy-washy cream puffs who campaigned on what ideas the polls said were popular with voters. Why run if you were going to be afraid of ticking off this interest group or that community? Jerry wanted to increase ballot access, encourage a high voter turnout, ensure quality education, and keep industry in Chicago so that the working class wouldn't be forced out of the city. He'd seen it happen: The wealthy gentrify a neighborhood; as a result, they don't want factories on their streets, so the developers force the factories to relocate in the suburbs; or, the cost of property is driven up, forcing the factories out of the cities and into cheaper locations. The city then becomes a dichotomy of rich and poor. How many hours had he spent talking with Roger Romanelli about that?

Roger graduated from Northwestern University, tucked into the safe, suburban folds of Evanston, north of Chicago—north, *north* of the South Side. In fact, the area was even called the North Shore. Well, Roger had gotten over that. He had spent the past six years working as an economic development organizer, trying to create a citywide policy on investing in human infrastructure. "Jobs aren't just about nickels and dimes," he would say in his quiet voice. "There's more than just the bottom line." But Roger wasn't a hipster urban frontiersman, slumming in community activism while living off a trust fund. He qualified as a twenty-eight-year-old true believer. "I want to make the whole world better," he told people, "but I live in Chicago. I'll start there." He cut an approachable figure, his face softened by a neatly trimmed brown beard and deep brown eyes framed with thick lashes. But Roger moved with intensity. He didn't get out of his car, he leaped. He didn't gesture, he jerked. The urgency gave away the thought that thrummed through his head every moment of the day: There wasn't a lot of time to play with. He worked for the 18th Street Development Company, two miles south of the Loop. It was one of the oldest areas of the city, the first section rebuilt after the Great Fire, and it had a lovely view of downtown Chicago. Now its buildings stood in bedraggled splendor, stained with soot and with paint peeling in curls.

This was opportunity, in Roger's eyes, but not for some real estate baron to sweep in and build condos. Instead, industry and residents could form a partnership. Roger thought this was the way to elevate a lower-middle-class neighborhood instead of throwing a few government dollars or hacking off blocks to developers, which was happening just a mile away in Chinatown. A retirement home went up, brick by brick. Roger knew what that meant: These new residents would start complaining about the few remaining factories, saying they blighted their view. The city government would listen like it always did and industry would end up leaving. Roger had watched it happen again and again, until he believed that the late Speaker of the House Tip O'Neill had been right when he said that all politics was local.

Old blood like Terry Gabinski would never change things. It would take a rogue campaign that put the fear of defeat in the establishment and then, down the road, would shake up the city in victory. There was the race for committeeman coming up. Nobody in Chicago ran for committeeman to *be* one, but to set himself up for another race. Jerry wanted to be alderman. *Shake it up, baby, shake it all up.* If he was going to do a serious run for alderman in 1999, he would need about $150,000 and name recognition. "You don't run the first time for anything in Chicago and expect to win," he told Roger.

It was John Henley, a thirty-three-year-old grassroots lobbyist, who suggested the committeeman spot in the Thirty-second Ward for a tryout. Not only did Jerry live there—always a good start—but the voter turnout was one of the lowest. "Gabinski has

*A NEW KIND OF PARTY ANIMAL*

a hard-core vote of only about four thousand," Henley said. "These precinct captains are in the business of counting on the innate laziness of voters. It's been so long since they've run a campaign on high voter turnout, it'll scare the hell out of them."

Jerry agreed wholeheartedly. "We're allowing a small group of senior citizen ward hacks," he said, "to elect someone to represent a majority young district."

So with $20,000 scraped from friends, unions, and himself, and with people like Roger Romanelli and John Henley on a 100-person, all-volunteer campaign staff, Jerry Morrison declared his candidacy for Democratic committeeman for the Thirty-second Ward of Chicago.

———

Just before Jerry made his announcement, Lead or Leave, an anti-deficit group aimed at young people, closed its doors. This didn't happen cleanly. First the phone was disconnected, then co-founders Rob Nelson and Jon Cowan seemed to disappear. Actually, Rob packed to go to law school while Jon scrambled for a job with the Clinton administration. They reemerged, in effect, only to turn off the lights.

The organization's members—mostly *former* members at this point—weren't too rattled. "Like we didn't expect it," muttered one, who joined right after the 1992 election and resigned after 1994. But the national media wavered between grieving for the loss of a child or scolding an errant one. Here they had just spent two years declaring Lead or Leave to be the Next Great Youth Movement in politics—putting Rob and Jon on the cover of *U.S. News & World Report* and on *60 Minutes,* quizzing them on *Nightline,* heralding them as "valiant spokesmen"—and what did Rob and Jon do? They quit.

The reporters who covered them had been dazzled by the rosy

glow they gave the political activism of their own youth. "A process of mass struggle involving much hard work and dedication . . . a legacy that everyone involved can justly be proud of," said one activist; "foot soldiers for democracy," declared a reporter. Well, actually, after the 1972 election, when the ballot was first extended to eighteen-year-olds, the voting percentage for 18–35s steadily dropped from a 49 percent high in presidential years to a 37 percent low. By comparison, forty-five- to sixty-four-year-olds, who voted at 70.8 percent in 1972, maintained a voting percentage of over 67 percent. The youth vote didn't go back up until 1992, when the people born before 1961 fully graduated from the "young American" category. The 1992 election saw, at 42 percent, the highest number of young voters since 1972. The memory is selective. These statistics never made it into any of the boomer retrospectives that bombarded the public throughout the 1990s. Then again, as *Vanity Fair*'s Christopher Hitchens wrote in 1996, " . . . most boomers didn't even do . . . sex, dope, [and] revolution. . . . They just think they did."

The press continued to map political involvement through placards and protests. When 18–35s didn't buy in to protesting as an effective tactic, the media stumbled, confused. This had to mean apathy, self-absorption, and whining—but then there was that nagging 42 percent figure. Obviously, young people voted. Since the 1972 youth vote had spokespeople like Hoffman and Rubin, the media figured, therefore, that today's youth would have a spokesperson, too. And because Hoffman and Rubin operated on the national level, that was where the media looked.

The first grasping attempts at generational—if not political— spokespeople included a sweat-soaked Eddie Vedder, fronting Pearl Jam, who glowered on the cover of *Time,* and actress Winona Ryder ("the Winona generation," *Rolling Stone* claimed). Thirty-one-year-old George Stephanopoulos proved useful for a while. The "boy wonder" of the White House so captured the

A NEW KIND OF PARTY ANIMAL

press that *The Washington Post* even chronicled his hair in a day-by-day diary. To many journalists, Stephanopoulos seemed to embody the youth movement that had swept Clinton into the White House. But as quickly as Stephanopoulos had enchanted the media, he fell out of favor. Besides blowing bubble gum during briefings, addressing reporters with an air of superiority they felt unbecoming to someone his age, and squiring actresses around town, Stephanopoulos was an insider. Hoffman, Rubin, and their cohorts had never been insiders.

Jon Cowan and Rob Nelson stood ready. When Lead or Leave held a protest in front of the American Association of Retired Persons headquarters, a gleaming building nicknamed "the Taj Mahal" by young Capitol Hill staffers, the press filmed the crowd throwing condoms into the air and shouting, "We're getting screwed!" Jon Cowan even called entitlements "our generation's Vietnam." Anyone who spoke to Jon could not doubt his sincerity: He squeezed his brow in lines to show his concern and tensed his voice with sternness. The veneer of packaging—the open-necked shirts, faded blue jeans, and cowboy boots—even worked. The twenty-six-year-old uttered lines like, "Bobby Kennedy was my hero . . . if there were another Vietnam War situation I'd want to be one of the people of my generation who know what to do about it."

Cowan never exactly explained what he would do about such a hypothetical, but that hardly mattered to the reporters who wrote about Lead or Leave. Vietnam, Kennedy, protests. Familiar territory at last! When Lead or Leave was launched in 1992, the most infamous photo, which landed on the cover of *U.S. News*, was Rob and Jon astride Rob's motorcycle, their arms folded in confident defiance as they grinned below the headline: "The Twentysomething Revolution That Will Change America." As an added bonus, Rob Nelson strutted in *his* blue jeans and cowboy boots, prompting a marketer to tell *New York* magazine that talking politics with Rob was "like talking politics with Marky Mark." Yes, *here* was the new youth movement in politics, and it made for delicious television.

The story of how they founded Lead or Leave varied, depending on the media venue. Sometimes they told reporters that it began as Rob's inspiration after he fell from an ice cliff and was saved by an angel, or after Rob and Jon met for happy hour and wrote up their master plan on a bar napkin, or after Rob and Jon met while climbing an ice cliff and then wrote their plan on a bar napkin. However they really came up with the idea, Rob and Jon were concerned about the deficit and thought somebody—namely, them—should be speaking about this on behalf of young Americans. When they approached Ross Perot for funding, he agreed with their premise. He donated $42,000 to their "lead us toward a lower deficit or leave office" cause. Rob and Jon immediately hired a Washington public relations firm. They told reporters that they wanted to make their peers aware of the deficit's generational unfairness.

The images of the two of them flickering across television screens inspired a slew of similar visages. All were well turned out in slacks and shirts carefully chosen to look nice on film. But their clean and quick replies weren't convincing. Down in Durham, North Carolina, Quillie Coath Jr., a twenty-seven-year-old juvenile diversion counselor, watched their television appearances and demanded, "Who died and left these people in charge?" These new talking heads sounded just like the older commentators. The only difference was that they had more hair and fewer wrinkles.

Rob and Jon considered themselves above the rest. They did have an organization, although the exact number of members was disputed. In their book, *Revolution X,* Rob and Jon claimed to have a "million-member grass-roots organization." They apparently crunched that number by adding up the number of students at every school affiliated with Lead or Leave. Twenty thousand was probably a more accurate count, still a large enough number to indicate a sense that 18–35s were desperate to get involved with politics, whether or not the issue they passionately cared about was the deficit. And actually, by 1996, they listed their top concerns as: the economy (24.5 percent), crime (18 percent), education (8 percent), and the environment (6 percent). These priorities remained steady through 1997 as well. By comparison, when the so-called foot soldiers for democracy were considered young America, they listed "nothing" as their top concern—polling 30 percent, far ahead of crime (11 percent) and education (8 percent).

Young people jammed Lead or Leave's phones, trying to join. Over 700 attended the Student Leadership Summit that Rob and Jon put on in Washington, D.C., in 1994. Jon predicted big things for the 1996 election. "I think ultimately what will happen, probably through Lead or Leave," he told a reporter, "is in ninety-six we'll have a Gen-X PAC that runs some young candidates, probably in a place like California, contesting congressional seats on a unified, cross-partisan ticket." Jon himself was a California native.

But, 18–35s were a diverse group. The deficit wasn't their only concern. Rob and Jon attempted to expand their platform and ended up with a rash of unfinished projects on their hands: "Register Once," a drive to increase college campus polling places; interactive educational software; and a national-debt rock concert to raise awareness about the deficit. This last one was held, but only because a different organization, The Fund to End the Deficit, put it on.

Lead or Leave's members got tired of tracking press coverage as their main involvement with the group. They wanted concrete action. And then stories started getting out: Rob and Jon wore shorts when they met with the chief of staff of the Senate Entitlements Commission; they didn't return members' phone calls because they were off on their book tour; they came to conferences shaded by purple sunglasses. This seemed gimmicky and unprofessional. Young people were having enough trouble in their attempts to be taken seriously by the establishment without two so-called spokesmen acting out every stereotype. And, some members questioned the cofounders' commitment. When Rob was asked during the Student Leadership Summit what he planned to do with Lead or Leave, he answered, "Well, I'm not going to be in nonprofit forever." Others wondered about his age. Rob had been twenty-eight when Lead or Leave started. For the past two years, in every article, he was identified as being twenty-nine. "Why wouldn't he be straight about his age?" asked a member. "It's not a big deal to us. It's a weird priority for them."

Weird priorities, deserted projects, twisted truths—18–35s could get that anywhere. Lead or Leave's members began to, well, leave. Staffers resigned. Donations dwindled. So in May 1995, very, very quietly, Lead or Leave shut down. Nelson went off to Stanford Law School, which he said he had deferred for two years, and Cowan landed a job at the Department of Housing and Urban Development. A bevy of groups salivated at the thought of stepping into the void and claiming former Lead or Leave members for their own. But that didn't happen. Why join another organization that seemed to be plunging into politics to get ahead themselves, not because they really cared? None had grassroots foundations. The key to all successful "special interest" groups is effective membership: educating them and organizing letter and phone campaigns. It takes years to build this action. But, following the Lead or Leave model, other youth groups wanted clout *now*— or, in lieu of this, at least the media attention. "[Their] future seems to lie in words, angry ones spewed out at the slightest provocation and fixed to hundreds of news outlets around the country," wrote the *Boston Globe*.

All talk, no action: The press settled comfortably into this assessment. But, following their own example once again, they never skimmed below the shiny surface of national politics. So they missed the real action, which was happening in the less-glamorous depths of the local levels.

A NEW KIND OF PARTY ANIMAL

Roger Romanelli first met Greg Gillam between shifts at WNUR, the student-run radio station at Northwestern University. Greg had run a tight radio show, every minute tapped and accounted for, which was how he now did his open-mike night at Sweet Alice. Open mikes happened all over Wicker Park, but Greg set his apart almost immediately. The beautiful people—even the artsy ones—usually drifted through the swankier thoroughfares of Lincoln Park or the Gold Coast, brushing against the starch and cashmere set. If they wanted to hear poetry, they went to the *official* poetry slam in Chicago, the one at the Green Mill, which practically had a trademark on the term. The guy who organized the contest also chaired the National Poetry Slam Competition and managed Chicago's poetry team, which was sponsored by . . . the Green Mill. No wonder Al Capone used to hang out there. Some things truly never changed.

People recited poetry at Greg's show, too, but he got around a potentially sticky situation with the poetry mavens at the Green Mill by calling it an open mike. An unusual number of gorgeous women seemed to show up at Sweet Alice on Tuesdays. They first came because they were friends of two of the people who worked there, and *they* happened to be ex-strippers. One even read her own poetry, and in Greg's opinion, nothing set the tone of an evening better than a statuesque woman reading stanzas about her breasts. Suddenly the show became very popular with a male clientele. The women eventually quit the bar (one to hang drywall), but their friends stayed. Men stayed because the women did. And once in their chairs, packed knee to elbow against chipped wooden bistro tables, this cross section of the younger population that lived in the Thirty-second Ward listened.

Roger knew all about the mess with Greg's former landlord and how Greg credited that with kicking him down the road that led to Sweet Alice, among other things. Greg, tall and lanky, his long brown hair pulled back, emceed the show in his softly manic voice. He already had a reputation on the poetry circuit, hosting a few open mikes and opening for bands. Once, a lesbian performance artist introduced him to an audience as "the only guy I'd go straight for." This about the guy who had grown up in Orlando and San Antonio suburbs, working at Sea World as Shamu one memorable summer. In bare feet, Greg was six one. In costume, he was a seven-foot walking Shamu. He didn't fool everybody. Once, a little kid cried, "You're not Shamu!" and punched Greg in the crotch as hard as he could. Now, finally, seven years later he was living the funky Bohemian urban existence he had wanted. But Greg had a political edge. He had become a canvasser extraordinaire.

Canvassers were all-important in any campaign, but especially in upstart ones. And Greg, well, he went into places sober that most people wouldn't wander into drunk. Uptown, a neighborhood just outside the Thirty-second Ward, had been his beat. The demographics were bizarre by any standard. Charity organizations like Hull House, and the Catholic Worker movement, had outreach branches there. A fundamentalist Christian group—"the Jesus People," Greg called them—had their main commune there. Across the intersection from a flophouse was a Buddhist temple. And a few streets away from "Blood Alley," where heroin users pushed rusting needles into collapsing veins, was an historic district where former Illinois Governor Jim Thompson had his Chicago home. Yuppies, ex-hookers, the disabled, and former junkies—Greg canvassed them all. He never seemed to do this with the candidates who were supported by the Democratic machine. As a result, his mailbox was vandalized so many times that he finally rented a post office box.

A guy like that, Roger thought, would be handy to have involved. He spotted Greg in the crowd at an arts festival in September 1995. Six months before, Roger had mentioned a possible swing at Terry Gabinski. Greg had said to let him know.

"We're doing it." Roger caught Greg by the arm. "We're making a run at Gabinski this winter."

"You're *what?*" Greg's jaw dropped. Sure, Roger had talked about it, but Greg knew a lot of people who *talked* about doing big things all the time. He was in the arts circle. People talked about writing novels, recording a CD, whatever, but they never actually *did* it. Greg found himself holding a shiny red foldout.

## IF YOU WERE IN CHARGE
## WHO WOULD YOU HIRE?

Help wanted: Committeeman for the 32nd Ward on city's near northwest side. Must be committed to rebuilding ward's voting power and to fair and open elections.

## ON ELECTION DAY, YOU ARE IN CHARGE. TAKE A LOOK AT THESE RÉSUMÉS BEFORE YOU VOTE.

Side by side were Gabinski's and Morrison's work records. Greg looked up in disbelief, and Roger smiled at him. "Have you met Jerry Morrison?" he asked. Greg considered himself savvy about slick-packaged politicians, but even he admitted that Jerry Morrison impressed the hell out of him. Jerry's handshake was solid, just like his thoughts. To Greg, the experienced canvasser, the most important aspect was that Jerry stood firm on running a campaign based on voter registration.

"Can we call on you?" Roger wanted to know as Jerry walked back over to his wife.

"Oh, yeah." Greg nodded vigorously. How unbelievably cool. A challenge to Gabinski!

Now that Greg knew, Roger expected the word-of-mouth campaign to start. Next came strategy. No matter what had happened in the 1992 national election, most of the younger set in Chicago did not vote in local elections. But then, their vote wasn't exactly cultivated, either. Every ward was divided into precincts, each of which had a captain. The party machine thoughtfully tailored the precincts to fit the abilities of every captain. As a result, there could be 100 people in one precinct and 700 in another, each captain armed with lists of voters. Their interest wasn't in turning out new ones. Precinct captains wanted to look good, and this meant, John Henley said, "bringing out the one hundred souls they've known for twenty years." In some precincts, 800 voters registered but only 150 turned out. And this was how elections were won. "There's no institutional pressure to get new voters," John added. "No one does anything because it's their *duty*. There've been studies by sociologists about World War II, why those guys fought so hard. It wasn't because they were more patriotic. It had to do with a sense of obligation to the four or five guys in their squad. They felt an obligation to not get each other killed."

If local elections didn't hinge on getting out the vote, neither did state and national elections. "The expediency of campaigning encourages both parties to narrow the pool that's voting," John said. He wasn't the only young person who thought this way. Growing up in an unprecedented age of television and technological development had cultivated a sophisticated sense of how government related on all levels. No one seemed to pick up on this because the media focused on national politics, only swooping to the local level during a scandal. Well, plenty happened before and after the arrest of Dan Rostenkowski. "People watch too much TV," Roger said. "Television says the important issues are the national issues. Politics is *local*."

When Jerry launched his campaign, the media and Terry Gabinski alike brushed him off. And why not, Gabinski hadn't even sent off any campaign mailings in at least twenty years. "Gabinski's gotten a bit lazy," John Henley said. "His troops have gotten lazy."

A NEW KIND OF PARTY ANIMAL

By his own count, Jerry had knocked on 5,000 doors as a community organizer. He believed face-to-face contact locked up a vote. "You know how hard that is these days?" he railed to Roger. "People live in gated communities, so you can't get to the door. They have answering machines, so they screen their calls. And they work, so they're never home." The Internet would be an ideal way to get around some of this, but it wasn't yet a viable option. For now, they would have to rely on direct mail and phone banks. "And voter registration," Jerry reminded his campaign team. "The more we register, the more we have to bring to the table." The point wasn't to win, but to accumulate clout. They had two months to do it.

Those two months happened to be January and February. And if 1996 was going to be anything like 1995, they had an enormous problem on their hands. That year, blizzard after blizzard had pounded the city, the wind chill dipping to fifty below zero as chunks of ice floated in Lake Michigan. Native Chicagoans wear their winters like a badge of courage, but people got frostbite in near-epidemic proportions. If you didn't get it, you lived in fear that you would. Greg had a scare when he had stepped into a half-frozen puddle while getting on a bus. His canvas sneakers and three layers of socks were soaked through and his feet became numb. When the man sitting next to him looked at his dripping shoe and said with pronounced authority, "Son, you're going to get frostbite on those toes," Greg headed straight for the emergency room. Yes, he admitted later, he had probably been a bit soft, especially when he watched paramedics carry in a man who clutched at his white-tipped ears, screaming bloody murder. But better safe than without toes. The winter of '95 spooked a lot of people— Greg included—before the first flake fell in '96. "People *die*," Greg said. "They lose body parts." And then Roger called him about canvassing—in January and February.

"I've got some ideas for you," Greg told him, "and I'll do what I can at the open mike."

He suggested registering voters at grocery stores. Roger set up the registration tables *inside*. The clerks would get on the public announcement system every fifteen minutes and announce that voter registration was happening in aisle five, or in the fruit section, or wherever they could make the space. The Morrison campaign registered over 1,000 people this way, no small achievement in a state notorious for its strict voter registration laws. "We registered people in almost every state," said Dave Anderson, production coordinator for MTV's Choose or Lose bus, which traveled across the country to raise voter awareness. "By far, the toughest place was Illinois. They're really trying to stop voter registration in large numbers."

Endorsements came next: Independent Voters of Illinois-Independent Precinct Organization, Illinois Public Action, Volunteer Precinct Organization, former alderman Dick Simpson. This last one was especially important. Dick Simpson had led a reform movement in the 1970s, going up against old man Daley's candidates and beating them. He had relied on an active electorate, creating "citizens congresses" that voted on issues he would be considering on the city council. With Simpson's approval locked up, Jerry's campaign was starting to look serious.

Then, another candidate asked to run a joint campaign with Jerry. Candidates often linked up this way to save on manpower and money. Richard Heathers was running for Illinois state representative. At thirty-seven, he wasn't much older than Jerry, but his campaign team had been in politics almost thirty years. When the two campaign staffs sat down for their first meeting, Jerry spent most of the time completely flabbergasted. All the Heathers guys could talk about was "changing the world"! Hello! he wanted to shout, what about *this* ward? Why don't we start *here?*

John Henley saw it differently. Sure, Heathers could be called a lakefront liberal, his head in the clouds. But he was a good guy. He had some solid people on his staff. Jerry just wanted to storm

Chicago as a regular, door-knocking Joe. So of course there would be a personality clash. "But that's irrelevant," John told Jerry. "What matters is what kind of resources you can pull together. We're going to have to fight unbelievably hard to make a decent run at this."

―――

The media rush to dissect 18–35s before the older half of the generation had grown into the full-blown adulthood of marriage, mortgage, and kids had a lot to do with the fact that politically at least, whatever profile develops in young people can have effects that ripple out beyond their age group once they come to power themselves. The twentysomethings in the 1890s called themselves a "galaxy and salvation army of military benevolence," bent on moral reform. By the mid-1920s, they had pushed through Prohibition and later led the call for intervention in World War II. Theodore Roosevelt's grandsons, who fought on the European front, would complain along with their peers that they were fighting another generation's battle. They would later start the Central Intelligence Agency, intending to circumvent such catastrophes. And, particularly, it was the young women of the flapper era who flexed newly won political clout as they physically challenged the nineteenth- and early-twentieth-century notion of females as fragile, fine china by sitting in speakeasies, sharing hip flasks in the backseats of parked cars, bobbing their hair, and shortening their skirts. In a way, the Eighteenth Amendment, which prohibited alcohol, brought about a more startling change in young American women than the Nineteenth Amendment, which gave them the right to vote. They mobilized against Prohibition, organizing several anti-Prohibition groups, including the Women's Organization for National Prohibition Reform, which within three years had over a million members. This was behavior that sent their mothers into near hysterics, not only because it was political but also because it was so unexpected.

But, the concept of cultivating youth to join a political party didn't catch on until midway through the twentieth century. The crux of advertising, a twentieth-century industry, is to get customers while they're young and keep them as customers for life. Political parties began to employ this same mentality in the 1960s. Barry Goldwater created a brigade of fresh-faced volunteers called "Goldwater Girls" (whose ranks included Hillary Rodham). But Richard Nixon went even further. In a 1968 speech to 10,000 in Anaheim, California, Nixon asked those in their twenties to raise their hands. When they did, he said, "What we are seeing here you see all over America. I want to say something. Today, too often we get the impression that the young people are going to the dogs. Today, too often, flashing across our television screen, we see the seamy side of American youth. Remember, I believe in young people. They are great. Give them a chance. That's what we want."

Nixon could not stress the importance of the youth vote enough. He watched uneasily as the Twenty-sixth Amendment, which extended the vote to eighteen-year-olds, made its way through Congress and around the states toward ratification in 1971. The most visible young Americans were Jerry Rubin and Abbie Hoffman, who had just written a book called *Vote!* It had chapters with titles like "Richard Nixon Is a Closet Queen." Somewhat understandably, according to a young campaign planner who met Nixon in 1971, "Nixon was uptight about the youth vote. That was his main concern then." So Nixon hired Kenneth Rietz to run the youth operation. Rietz was thirty and he looked even younger—an unaged face for the untried vote. More than 125,000 volunteers worked for Young Voters for the President, registering voters and passing out campaign material. Rubin dismissed them (regardless of gender) as "Nixonettes": "Each one lean and tall, as tall as an elephant's eye. With Ultra-Brite teeth and Pristine crotches. With Maidenform bras and the kind of heavy, shiny shoes you store in the closet rack with presses—Florsheims, no doubt. Everybody looks like Tricia Nixon or David Eisenhower."

But Nixon made a specific promise to young voters: that he would end the war in Vietnam and then abolish the draft and create an all-volunteer army. To a generation whose biggest concern (at least at that time) was the draft, that sounded pretty good. Nixon received about 57 percent of the youth vote in 1972. Twenty-four years later his "Young Voters for the President" campaign buttons would be selling for twenty bucks in antiques stores, but the seeds had been sown. The majority of those born between 1945 and 1960 would continue to vote Republican, even giving Ronald Reagan his largest percentage of support in 1980 and 1984. The Republican National Committee built the College Republicans into the largest political group for young Americans. By the 1980s, the College Republicans would even be the biggest student group at the University of California at Berkeley—something virtually unthinkable ten years earlier. No wonder Jerry Rubin ended up on Wall Street.

Reagan took his cue from Nixon and had his own visible, young lieutenants like Mari Maseng in public liaison, and Gary Bauer in domestic policy (both went on to high-profile positions in the conservative movement). Even less senior but highly ambitious politicians like Newt Gingrich had long included young people in their plans. "I've actually thought since I was a student at Emory that we needed to target young people on a long-term basis," Gingrich says. "Young people are always looking at which candidate represents the best way for their future, and I've always thought that Republicans had to make our case to young people." This was not a secret. By 1992, *The Washington Post* admitted that "young voters [are] the linchpin of long-range Republican strategies."

By the time the Republicans took over Congress in 1994, the GOP recruits from the past twenty years had built an amazingly well-oiled, nurturing machine. Morton Blackwell, former chairman of the Virginia Republican Party, started the Leadership Institute, a training school for young conservatives. Burton Yale Pines, chairman of the right-wing National Center for Public Policy Research, and Paul Weyrich, chairman of the conservative National Empowerment Television, cohosted lunch every Wednesday for young conservatives in Washington. And Grover Norquist, president of Americans for Tax Reform, threw weekly cocktail parties at his Capitol Hill town house for young Republican staffers.

The GOP made itself visible on state and local levels, too. Kim Alexander, the thirty-year-old executive director of the nonpartisan educational California Voter Foundation, alternated between amazement and frustration as she watched the efforts on the West Coast. "It's unbelievable—they've got young people out there every day registering people to vote, passing out literature, holding informational meetings," she said, shaking her head. "The Democrats have nothing like it here. I go to their meetings, and they've only got old people there. What kind of future is that?"

———

Jerry was starting to ask that same question. Every time he met with Richard Heathers, he wanted to pound his head into the wall. If Jerry had thought the first meeting was bad, that was nothing compared to the continual attempt to shove warm and fuzzy, touchy-feely philosophy down his throat. Why the hell were they discussing philosophy when they needed to talk organization! And Heathers's staff made no secret of the condescension they felt for the new bucks on the scene. *They* had done this sort of thing since the sixties. "Oh yeah? Well, *we* have already out-fund-raised *you*," Jerry returned. He couldn't get over that. Richard Heathers had been around politics for years, and Jerry had kicked him in the coffers.

Richard Heathers wanted to put the five people he had for the Thirty-second Ward in charge. Jerry's forty volunteers could work under his people, Richard explained. "You've got five people in the Thirty-second Ward and I've got forty," Jerry repeated. "Why the hell are we dealing with you, anyway? You're getting a sweet-ass deal. I'm not fitting my volunteers into your plan. I'm putting them out in the field."

John Henley groaned when he heard about this. Heathers was in a tough race—against a well-connected figure. The last thing he needed was a personality tiff. And Jerry had bigger problems, too. In a sort of backhanded compliment, Terry Gabinski sent out campaign literature. Incumbents didn't do that in Chicago unless they felt threatened. Gabinski even labeled Jerry as a carpetbagger because of his southeast childhood. A carpetbagger! Jerry now lived on the 2200 block of Iowa. When his great-grandfather had emigrated from Poland in the early 1900s ("Morrison" was technically a Welsh name but you don't grow up Welsh if you were 50 percent Polish and lived in Chicago), he had first moved to the 2400 block of Iowa. The thing about old Chicago families was that they never forgot where they came from. The closer the Democratic primary came—which, in Chicago, is as good as Election Day itself—the weirder things got. Gabinski supporters spit on Roger's car when he parked at Morrison campaign headquarters. "Communist!" they shouted as he got out. "Carpetbagger!" Others were shoved around when they tried to put up Morrison signs. "Typical Chicago intimidation stuff," John Henley calmly observed.

And then, Sweet Alice closed down. Greg Gillam couldn't believe it. Not because just the previous week one of the guys from Urge Overkill had stopped by to check out the open mike and had asked, "Mind if I come back next week and play some stuff I want to try out?" No, Greg was floored because Sweet Alice's owner, who was Chicago born and bred and had already lost one bar, had neglected to renew his entertainment license since 1993. The owner and head manager both seemed to have no political acumen whatsoever. They didn't physically go down to city hall and stand in lines and talk to the right people to find out what was wrong and then how to renew the license. Greg did. "I was patient and respectful and polite, and I got the answers I needed," he told Roger. "They're so inept, they didn't find out anything." Once again, as Greg pointed out to anyone who would listen, it paid to know the local ropes.

It was cold and windy on election day in March 1996. Snow was still piled up from the last storm. Jerry shook his head. Bad weather never helped voter turnout. Sure enough, less than 30 percent showed up. Still, Jerry and John Henley spent most of their day running around, putting out fires. A police officer wanted to arrest a Morrison volunteer for passing within 100 feet of a voting booth. One election monitor, who was part of the Gabinski organization, wanted to take the ballots from the locked ballot box and put them into her purse and drive to election head-quarters to count them—without taking a Morrison volunteer with her. John shook his head. Yeah, *right*. A volunteer jumped into the monitor's car, anyway.

Jerry took 30 percent. He was delighted. That equaled nearly 3,000 votes. In Chicago terms, Jerry Morrison was now a player. His 1999 campaign for alderman was *on*. According to John Henley's estimates, Jerry needed 2,000 more votes to knock off Gabinski. "That all depends on how hard you're willing to work," John told him.

Jerry's allies among the independent set had begun to organize as well. In 1999, they wouldn't run just Jerry for office. They would put up six to eight candidates in the hope of creating a base. From there, they could run for a congressional seat. An alternative ward association was possible. The Northwest Political Organization and the Abbey Group, which combined like-minded young Republicans and Democrats, agreed. "It's going to take hundreds of efforts like ours to change things," Jerry said. "One huge effort on the national level isn't going to do it."

Meanwhile, the media continued to pound away. "The much ballyhooed 'Gen X' crowd," griped *O'Dwyer's Washington Report*, "needs a good sock in the jaw when it comes to interest in public affairs."

## Chapter Two

# *OPEN COMMITMENT*

*Among democratic nations, each generation is a new people.*

—Alexis de Tocqueville,
*Democracy in America*
(1835)

About the time Jerry Morrison decided to run for committee-man, Bob Meagher finally questioned the sanity of Lynn Marquis. True, this was generally a precious commodity in Washington, but Bob was starting to think all Democrats were nuts. He'd only said, "Welfare reform isn't really cutting welfare," and Lynn had thrown her glass of beer on him—a *full* glass. Of really good beer. And the day before, I had nearly broken my hand, clocking him in the halls of the Capitol. Privately, Bob chalked it all up to PMS, but he tugged at his soaked shirt and shouted above the cracking cue balls and clattering beer glasses, "You're taking this way too seriously!"

Bardo's had seen fights before, but probably none over welfare reform. The clusters of college students around us stared, as if we had just dropped down from Mars (no, worse, Capitol Hill). Lynn blinked furiously to keep from crying. She teared up whenever she got really mad, and that only made her even angrier. How simpering. How weak. She would rather flush purple, like Bob did across the sticky table. I drank the rest of my beer. Here we had gone to down a couple of pitchers at the cavernous bar just across the Key Bridge in Virginia to escape the Hill, and all we could dish was politics. Most congressional staffers really did have lives beyond policy talk, but the bitterness of the welfare reform debate stung until we oozed with rhetoric.

It was only three years ago that this happened, but in your twenties that seems like a whole different era. In 1,095 yesterdays, we would find the events that shaped the dominating force of our emerging political character. What occurred in 1995 would ensnare most of the twenty-two- to thirty-five-year-olds who were in Washington at the time and leave an indelible imprint on their minds.

This was crucial if politics really, truly was to change. According to the usual game that was played in Washington, our bosses, the members of Congress, slugged it out along party lines. The older staffers, the ones over thirty-seven, fought along party lines. And when the welfare debate broke in 1995, it looked like the younger staffers would also trip down the well-worn partisan path. The establishment conveniently dismissed the fact that most of the eighteen- to thirty-five-year old electorate did not identify with either the Republicans or the Democrats. One would think that when the largest potential voting-age bloc leans independent that the two major parties would start asking hard questions, like

A NEW KIND OF PARTY ANIMAL

*why*. But that didn't even register with them, mainly because the numbers of young independents began increasing around the time of the welfare battle, when the most immediate reference to young people that congressmen had was their own staffers, and *they* certainly didn't seem post-partisan with episodes like the one at Bardo's erupting on a regular basis.

Actually, though, the young Hill staffers (average age twenty-six) weren't so different from their peers. They had come to Capitol Hill bragging about voting mixed tickets—some were even registered as independents—and breaking the cardinal rule of not chatting across party lines. But when the welfare battle began, well, all that went out the window. Some of the older staffers called it the "come-to-Jesus" moment. "It happens to everyone," Joe Morgan once muttered as he poured Jack Daniel's into a twelve-ounce plastic cup packed with ice. He had spent twelve years on the Hill, so he subscribed to the old school of keeping a bottle handy at the bottom of a desk drawer. "You come here, you think you're going to change the world. Then something happens that makes you realize the best you can do is go along with everything. And then you either accept this and stay, or you don't and you leave."

Joe, at thirty-seven, was typical of the old guard. His "come-to-Jesus" moment had been so inconsequential that he didn't even remember it anymore. Or maybe he'd lost it in the alcoholic haze that had drifted with him since the '70s. His eyes were folded behind puffs of skin and his face was stained a mottled red. He had his slice of power. After working slowly, painfully up the rungs of a congressional staff—from assistant to legislative correspondent to legislative aide to legislative director to, finally, chief of staff—Joe was a known entity on the Hill. He was known as a guy who could get in a fight in an empty room. That was a useful reputation to have in Washington. Joe relished it.

As part of the tried-and-true entrenched, he parroted party

agenda. His peers had come in in an era when lunch could be swilled in martini glasses and dinner could be pounded in shots. Deals were cut in dark bars and the right dirty joke got more mileage than a Japanese car. This was the system, at least until the early 1990s. By then, thanks to journalistic damnation of government excess, the frills had been trimmed to a cocktail circuit that boasted greasy mini-quiches and cheap wine. But the back-slapping, spine-stiffening party loyalty remained. Aside from polite schmoozing when necessary, Republicans and Democrats did not do business. Period.

Then, around January 1993, the Hill scene began to shift. At first, nothing seemed unusual. A whole new crop of fresh-faced college graduates from every corner of the nation hit town, droolingly eager to land an $18,000-a-year, eighteen-hour-a-day job. This ritual had gone on for at least thirty years. Once they were hired, they would stay an average of three years. If history repeated itself, they would go back to their home states and become state and county party chairmen, consultants, teachers, and activists. Sure, some would-be politicos arrived, lusting for national power. That was part of the ritual, too. But early on, there were signs that the new group might be different. One case became particularly infamous. Ol' Sport was a beefy slab of a guy who liked to wear cowboy boots with shiny suits. He was only twenty-one but claimed then–White House Chief of Staff Leon Panetta and Redskins owner Jack Kent Cooke as his "good friends." He also said he was the executive director of the Democratic Caucus, which sounded impressive except that the Democratic Caucus didn't have an executive director. But, as it ended up, he did work there—as an unpaid intern. His act didn't last long. While unpaid interns could shoot their mouths off to older politicos and get away with it—sometimes even with grudging admiration—his peers had no patience. The aftermath of the Republican takeover proved to be an excellent reason for the intern coordinator, age

A NEW KIND OF PARTY ANIMAL

twenty-seven, to dismiss him. Last anyone heard, Ol' Sport was tending bar in Virginia, telling customers he had turned down a paying job with the caucus so that "the party could keep the money." The story made the rounds and probably sounded swell to the suit crowd. Loyalty! Commitment! His own peers didn't bite. "You have *got* to be kidding me," said a twenty-four-year-old aide who worked for the caucus. "Spin, spin, spin. He doesn't really expect *us* to believe that, does he?"

Still, the brief once-over that most people gave Hill staffers brought out the ideologues who were violently left or right. Those were the ones who got the attention. Then again, they were the easiest to identify and understand *and* they fit perfectly with the times. When Bill Clinton was elected in 1992, the media touted the "rise of hip young Democrats." Two years later, when the Republicans took over Congress for the first time in forty years, "Young Conservative Chic" became all the rage. *The New York Times Magazine* put them, snarling in their suspenders and miniskirts, on the cover. And *Cigar Aficionado* even did a photo spread with several aides, all dressed in black and puffing on their favorite brands. The poster conservatives included journalist David Brock, who kept a bumper sticker on a table in his front hallway that read, "President Gore—Don't Pardon Hillary" (by 1997, Brock would be posing in *Esquire,* chained to a tree, claiming to be a victim of the rabid conservatives he once consorted with); sometime lawyer and fledgling media monster Laura Ingraham; Horace Cooper, legislative counsel to House Majority Leader Dick Armey; and Kevin Pritchett, a former editor of *The Dartmouth Review* who now worked as a floor assistant to Senator Trent Lott.

But floating beyond the gray haze, a barely perceptible change began to unsettle the older aides like Joe Morgan. "What the hell is going on?" Joe demanded, stomping down the hall after seeing a Republican staffer laughing with a Democrat. "Haven't these guys ever heard: us, them; us, them. That's how it works!" So when the Republican Congress made its first attempt at welfare reform, Joe watched with no small amount of glee as it became the "come-to-Jesus" moment not just for me, or Lynn, or Bob, or even Robert George, who skipped Bardo's that night because he was stuck over in the Speaker's office, but for a chunk of the 8,000 aides working on the Hill then. Now, Joe was convinced, the little upstarts would fall into line with the party just as every generation ahead of them had.

———

President Clinton could not logistically go to each inaugural ball in 1993—there were twelve, scattered throughout Washington, attended by people who had given hundreds of dollars to see him in that tuxedo. But he made a point to stop by the MTV Ball long enough to say, "Everybody knows MTV had a lot to do with the Clinton-Gore victory. One of the things that I am proudest of is the record number of young people who voted and put us in."

Four years later, at the Youth Ball (MTV opted to throw a cocktail party instead), Clinton did not make an appearance but Al Gore did. "The young people of America," the vice president announced to the crowd, "gave Bill Clinton and me this election!" This was a strange statement to make. If anything, the results of the '92, '94, and '96 elections should have caused Gore, who badly wants the Democratic nomination in 2000, to do a double take.

The signs were there from 1992 that something was different about the 18–35s, even though over 40 percent of them had voted for Clinton that year. Consultants assumed that this group fell according to the standards of older voting blocs. People fifty and older tend to support candidates based on party affiliation. Those between thirty-six and forty-nine base their vote on a politician's good character (or lack thereof). But in the rush to hail "hip young

Democrats," Ross Perot's showing with young people went all but overlooked. Perot won 22 percent of the eighteen to thirty-five vote in 1992, his strongest of any age bloc. Then, in a twist to the establishment's line of reasoning, between 1993 and 1994 third parties suddenly saw their rosters expand fast and noticeably. The Libertarian Party increased by 20 percent. The Green Party, established in California in 1990, had 100,000 on its rosters, enough to land a spot on the state's ballot. When organizers of both parties checked their rosters, they found that a majority of new members were 18–35s. Kim Alexander made it part of her job at the California Voter Foundation to register her peers to vote. In 1992, most of them signed up as Democrats. In 1994, they asked her, "Do I have to register Democratic or Republican, or can I make up something else?" Yes, this was just one state, but it happened to be the largest in the nation, with 54 electoral college votes. And it just so happened that a higher percentage of 18–35s went to the polls in 1992 than even senior citizens, who traditionally vote in the highest percentage.

In Texas, the second-largest state (in terms of electoral college votes, and even then Texans consider that a sketchy standard), the news was just as strange. By 1994, over 70 percent of registered Democrats in the primaries were over age sixty-five. But the Republican rosters hadn't swelled. The Reform Party, Libertarian Party, and Green Party had. In 1996, though, the Reform Party would lose ground among 18–35s across the country. The Reform Party remained the Perot Party, eschewing legitimate leadership and declining to support like-minded congressional candidates in the midterm election. Besides, Perot had started to look like every other politician. With quips and graphs, he could articulate problems, but he rarely laid out solutions. That wasn't "changing government as we know it," as he had promised. That was the same old game.

Many politicos still brushed off the rising independents in California and Texas. For one thing, those states are not considered part of the "Middle America" that elected officials are so fond of referring to, being marked by trendy clothes, big hair, and auras. A state like, say, Massachusetts couldn't be lumped in with them. Massachusetts had baked beans, turtlenecks, and the Puritans' sense of sin. No wonder that by the 1996 Democratic convention, the Massachusetts delegation would be reeling from the news that—for the first time ever—over 50 percent of voters were registered as independents. "We have no idea what's going on," said Harold Naughton Jr., state representative from the Twelfth Worcester District, "except that a lot of it is because of young people." The Libertarian Party, though, was delighted to learn that the Boston area had become one of its largest bases of fundraising.

If 18–35s were hedging their bets on committing to a party, they were also hesitant to embrace a single ideology. Despite the increase in coverage in 1995 of young conservatives, the electorate did not exactly rush the elephant. Thirty-seven percent of 18–35s considered themselves conservative, but an equal number claimed to be moderate. When it came to actually punching the ballot, less than one-fourth voted straight party lines.

Again, the Democratic and Republican parties pretty much dismissed all this, especially after 18–35s voted in such low numbers in 1994. The youth vote wasn't reliable. And then the surge in eighteen- to thirty-five-year-old independents meant that they were unpredictable, to boot. As Jerry Morrison tried to exploit in his race against Terry Gabinski, the political establishment dislikes the unpredictable. Its dirty little secret is that it *prefers* a low turnout. "Over the years, consultants have finessed elections so much that they now can identify exactly how many votes a candidate needs, where those votes are, and how to get them," says Kimberly Schuld, a thirty-year-old former political consultant and vice president of The Polling Company. "They train their candidates to speak to the people that are in that equation and that equation only." The political establishment would rather see a tough fit like the 18–35s stay home than show up to vote. And for a while, it seemed as if politicos were going to get this wish.

A string of scandals has left both major parties fallible: the memories of Vietnam and Watergate that were dredged up by a media that had witnessed them, and other events more contemporary with 18–35s, like Iran-Contra, the S & L crisis, Anita Hill, Whitewater, and Monica Lewinsky. Neither party has ever been seen by young people as being remotely honorable. Many also grew up hearing the same line my mother always used with me: "You just have to accept the lesser of two evils." That isn't exactly positive reinforcement. Between 1992, when 18–35s found out they could vote in large numbers, and 1994, when 18–35s came two years closer to being the largest potential voting-age bloc, they began asking: Why do you always have to be choosing the lesser of two evils? Why can't you demand the best for the job? And if the best person for the job wasn't a Democrat or a Republican, *why not support another party?*

In 1994, Clinton wasn't looking like the best man. Many 18–35s felt he dismissed them with candy. He talked about wearing briefs instead of boxers. When he stumped at Ohio State University, the most populous campus in the country, he left the audience exasperated. "He talked about education loans and our football team," complained a student. They wanted to hear about jobs, the deficit, and crime. By the beginning of 1996, over 60 percent of young people did not believe Clinton represented their views or understood their needs.

They weren't so disillusioned that they didn't register to vote. During the first four weeks of Rock the Vote's register-by-phone campaign, the organization received 75,000 calls on its 800 number. Over 10,000 young voters registered at Lollapalooza. The MTV Choose or Lose bus traveled the country and registered

37,000 new voters. And 40 percent of the 12 million new voters brought in through Motor Voter were under twenty-nine. Making a tenuous situation even worse, as far as the Democratic and Republican parties were concerned, just before the 1996 election nearly 70 percent of 18–35s said they would like to vote for a third-party candidate for president.

By this point, the Capitol Hill scene—the one beyond swanky cocktail parties in Georgetown and state dinners at the White House—had already begun to rumble through its own post-partisan shift.

———

Bob Meagher—pronounced "Ma-har" ("There's nothing 'meager' about me," he says)—threw his wingtips into his black car and took off for Washington the second he graduated from college. He'd heard Washington was full of single, smart women. That fit his immediate requirements. So he left the shimmering heat and flying cockroaches of the Deep South for the occasional snow and seventeen-year cicadas of the Mid-Atlantic region. The cicadas crawled out of the ground upon his arrival to mate for a month and then die. Bob didn't quite know how to take this. He didn't *really* believe in omens. Then, the first day of his job search, Bob walked out the door, a hundred résumés in hand, and the first thing he saw was the headline blazing across *USA Today:* WORST JOB MARKET FOR COLLEGE GRADS EVER. Well. Take that with your Post Toasties.

The typical job search could last two weeks to six months, depending on how willing you were to start at entry level. Bob wanted to be a legislative aide, a senior position. Every congressperson employed at least three to track certain issues. But between the cicadas and the newspaper headline, "staff assistant" was starting to sound just fine.

*A NEW KIND OF PARTY ANIMAL*

He knocked on every Republican door until a member from Florida offered him a data entry job from nine until noon for $13,000. Bob took it. You do what you have to do, he reasoned. And from three to ten, he scooped ice cream at—where else?—Bob's Ice Cream over on the Senate side. It was only six bucks an hour, but he could eat all the ice cream he wanted. He did this for about four months before the congressman offered him a full-time job as a legislative correspondent, writing letters to constituents.

Just as Bob settled into the Washington routine (into the office at seven-thirty, lunch at his desk, rounds of cocktail parties at six, back to the office by eight, and home by eleven), Lynn Marquis wore out three pairs of heels on Independence Avenue pounding the proverbial pavement. She wanted to work on the House side. Sure, over on Constitution Avenue, the Senate came with fancy trimmings like mahogany paneling and stamped-leather wall coverings. But Senate staffers had to adhere to strict roles. The legislative aides waited years to write bills. On the House side, well, anything could happen. Congressmen liked to say its frenetic energy made it "the People's house." Lynn thought it was more of a mosh pit. And somewhere in all that bouncing around, the aides got responsibility fast. Lynn wanted in on that game, and who could call this impatience when the House staffer who wrote deficit reduction into the budget was only a year older than she was.

No one in Biddeford, Maine, expected Lynn to go to Washington. Biddeford, a blue-collar town spitting distance from blue-blooded Kennebunkport, sent its sons and daughters to college. Then they came home. There was no indication that Lynn would be any different. She was the youngest and the only girl in the squarely middle-class Marquis family. And as far as her older brothers were concerned, because she was the youngest and the only girl *and* armed with big baby blues, she got away with everything. High school blurred into parties. Lynn didn't give two minutes to her future, until her high school civics teacher told her she had a mind for politics. She should go to Washington, her teacher said, and see if she could cut it. Why not, Lynn thought breezily. She had visited the city once, as part of a junior high school trip. It seemed interesting enough. But when it came to plotting the move all through four years at Southern Maine University, she got serious. She took all the necessary classes, volunteered on campaigns, thought about law school, and left soon after graduation.

Like Bob, Lynn wanted to be a legislative aide. Unlike him, she wanted to work for a Democrat. Earth Day was a national holiday on her calendar, even if she did grow up in a Republican household. The Democrat she ended up with was a pro-gun, anti–Earth First Oklahoman, but then Lynn landed in the WORST JOB MARKET FOR COLLEGE GRADS EVER. When Bill Brewster, an affable pharmacist by trade, offered her a position as a computer systems aide with the promise of the first legislative slot that came open, Lynn jumped at it.

Brewster's office was in the Longworth House Office Building, just across the street from the Capitol. There was nothing glamorous about it. The congressional offices probably violated every safety code in the book, overcrowded and stuffed with volumes of paper. Dust floated in such quantities that staffers who wore contact lenses all kept bottles of saline handy. And the elevators—those had been voted the "worst of Capitol Hill" almost every year that the Hill newspaper, *Roll Call*, asked the question. Besides creaking threateningly, sliding like snails through the shafts, and frequently jamming between stops, the elevators tended to violently drop several floors at once. They would never be renovated, though. The public hated it when Congress voted itself funds for that sort of thing. Someone would have to die before constituents would relent, and even then that unfortunate person had better be a tourist. "If a member or a staffer dies," Lynn sighed, "they'd just say, 'good riddance.'" She was only half joking.

Longworth stood in the middle of the three House office

buildings. Bob and I worked in the newest one, Rayburn. It was a marble monstrosity constructed with all the charm of the 1950s. Everyone—tourists, staffers, even members—got lost in the double-H shape of the building. The cold whiteness of the floor, ceiling, and walls gave off all the cheeriness of a mausoleum. Bob maintained that there was a good chance that air from 1954 was still being recirculated. "All the windows are hermetically sealed," he said. "Who knows what's still floating around here?"

Then, there was Cannon. The oldest House office building boasted wide marble halls, frosted lighting fixtures, and stair banisters that curved in bronze curls. Cannon screamed, "This is Congress!" And Robert George worked there as if he'd been born to it. He might have looked younger than thirty-four, with his round face and wide eyes, but he had enough political acumen to end up at the dinner table of GOP diva Arianna Huffington.

He wore tailored—but never flashy—suits and walked energetically, always leaning forward. A black Catholic born in the West Indies and reared by a single, work-to-the-bone mother wasn't exactly standard Republican fare. But Robert had never been one for tidy categorizing. Raised in England, New York City, and northern California, he went to college in Maryland. In between his parents split up twice, and once he landed in a foster home outside London while his mother tried to paste together a nursing career.

Robert fell into the Republican ranks when a neighbor offered him a volunteer job at the 1988 Republican National Convention. He saw politics as pieces of issues, not a sweeping platform. Unfortunately, this was not in vogue when Robert first came to Washington. When he dished his standard line—"I'm very accepting of certain viewpoints and intolerant about intolerance"—people usually stared, open-mouthed. The mores of the time dictated that he had to choose a party, not just a philosophy. Since he agreed enough with the Republicans, he went with them. By 1995, Robert had moved out of Cannon and into the Capitol itself, writing editorials for Speaker Gingrich. MTV News promptly offered him a spot on their 1996 campaign team. The idea appealed to him briefly. Outside the Speaker's office, Robert earned extra money by working as a deejay. MTV could have been a chance to be around the kings of deejays. But he realized pretty early on that he'd be the token Republican on the news staff. "How 'bout that," he said, bemused. "The Republican who's against affirmative action benefits from it." Robert turned them down. It wasn't so much a partisan issue as a career decision, since he had been with the Speaker for less than a year. He couldn't leave yet.

The Hill was a tight world, so maybe the four of us would have run into each other eventually. If your bosses were on the same committees, or if you played on one of the congressional office softball teams, or if you drank at certain bars, you were bound to strike up some sort of bond. In our case, we met through Third Millennium. It was one of the many so-called political advocacy groups for young Americans that had sprung up in the wake of Lead or Leave. Third Millennium had carefully declared itself nonpartisan, which was the main reason we wandered into it in 1993, right after it was started. Its headquarters were in New York because most of its founders were New Yorkers. This was great for media accessibility, but bad for political clout. Then again, almost immediately, it became apparent that this suited Third Millennium just fine. Instead of cultivating membership, it poured its limited resources into polls. "If we release the polls, we get press, and that leads to more money," the twenty-nine-year-old executive director said. Press clippings didn't get policy done, though. Bob, Lynn, and I decided to use our limited free time in other ways. We resigned from the organization after two years. Robert continued to pay dues, but that was about it.

Like most young staffers, we stayed friendly even once the Republicans took over in 1994. ("Republican Party, I wish you well," said Congressman Jim Traficant on the House floor—staffers usually stopped whatever they were doing to listen to the Ohio Democrat's wild speeches—"May you never be hated by Tonya Harding and never be loved by Lorena Bobbit.") Bob was a legislative director at this point, and Lynn had been promoted to legislative aide. Notwithstanding shifting jobs, and, at times, political affiliations, we stayed close—discussing information and issues of the day. This was the norm, and it shouldn't have surprised anyone, especially considering that a majority of these aides had cut their political teeth on health care reform.

The very words "health care reform" had eye-glazing potential, except that when the White House introduced its plan in 1994, it was very clear about who would pay the bill. "Yeah, your most pissed-off group about this is going to be the young, healthy singles," said then–White House consultant Mandy Grunwald, tossing her dark hair. She was briefing Democratic press secretaries, right before the plan's release, to keep them "on message."

"They're the ones who're going to have to pay for it," she continued, "but they'll get over it. Our strongest supporters are young people."

She must have been oblivious to the fact that she was addressing an audience full of young, healthy singles—not to mention the kind of young, healthy singles who liked nothing better than to rifle through thick policy language to figure out what the hell she meant by "pay for it." And there it was: "community rating," which lumped together everyone—young, old, healthy, sick—and charged a single fee. This was a bargain for the elderly, since they used health care over 300 times more than the average healthy person did. But, it literally knocked young people out of the system. When New York State passed it in 1993, tens of thousands of people under thirty-six dropped their health insurance—one large insurer, Mutual of Omaha, lost 43 percent of its New York customers while its policyholders' average age rose 3.4 years. Young people couldn't afford it, not when their premiums rose 170 percent (while sixty-year-old men enjoyed a 45 percent cut). And there again, the White House had anticipated this. Its plan made participation mandatory.

Since there was no viable grassroots group for young people—Hill staffers had brushed off Lead or Leave long before it even folded, and Third Millennium didn't have enough members to be influential beyond a few sound bites—congressional aides saw themselves as the de facto watchdogs in Washington. Democratic aides passed copies of the plan on to Republican staffers. The more mathematically inclined tried to crunch the numbers themselves, just to see who was right: the White House, which claimed the plan would cost $59 billion; or the nonpartisan Congressional Budget Office, which said $74 billion.

"I guess this is as good a time as any to remind you that President Johnson thought Medicare would only cost nine billion dollars by 1990," Bob said to Lynn. She glared at him darkly, but she didn't argue. She handled Medicare in her office. She knew it now racked up costs of $66 billion.

Press secretaries on both sides brought up community rating to reporters. The media, desperately searching for some sexy angle, asked the president about it. "I think most healthy, single Americans would be willing to do that to avoid the kind of horror stories we've heard," Clinton said. And the barest complaint by young people about community rating was roundly disparaged by senior citizens. *The New York Times* ran their letters: "I pay for schools with my taxes and I don't use them, so you can pay for my health care!"

Bob rolled his eyes in disgust. "When was the last time you ever heard a senior happily go with a tax increase to pay for schools?" he asked.

So health care reform established enough siegelike camaraderie among young aides to make older staffers like Joe Morgan wonder when they were going to get with the program like everybody else. "Don't any of you know the meaning of party lines?" he once demanded. That was what the "100 Days" was all about. The media recorded every move and bitter word of politicians. Then many of them—reporters and members alike—wrote books about it. But none ever picked up on the battle just below, the one that would reverberate beyond a mere age group and would affect politics for decades to come.

At first, the Republican takeover didn't faze young aides. Lynn even remarked optimistically, "It might be good to shake things up." Older Hill staffers barely suppressed their dismay. "They're gonna screw us like we screwed them," said Joe Morgan. He was so much the Democrat that he owned ties dotted with donkeys. He also had little else in his life than the stack of papers that covered his desk. The woman he thought he loved had left him two years before to "go find herself," she told him. He never visited his family—they lived in the frosty wilds of New Hampshire. When his mother came to visit, Joe was conveniently off on a junket to Asia.

The Republican takeover primarily affected his flow of freebies. As a chief of staff, Joe had cleaned up when the Democrats had ruled. Bottles of wine and whiskey rattled through the office during Christmas. A daily offer for hockey or baseball or whatever tickets were in season almost always came his way. But when the Republicans came to power, the lobbyists didn't need Joe as much. The flow ebbed. His anger climbed. This was *not* how things were supposed to be, not at his age, not in his position. So when Joe happened to see a fax come over from a Republican leadership office (the cover sheet read, "Thanks for your help—hope you find this useful"), he nearly burst a vein.

"Goddammit—we're supposed to be fighting against them, not talking to them!" he shouted, brandishing the fax like a weapon. "That's the way it works around here." He stormed back to his desk, muttering under his breath that we, like everyone who came before us, "would learn."

Then, welfare reform struck, smack in the middle of the so-called 100 Days. Whatever usefulness that title had given Franklin Roosevelt when he coined it in 1932, it was now gone as far as staffers were concerned. "One hundred days of no sleep," Bob called it. Eighteen-hour days, six days a week. We didn't creep into work at 7:30 A.M. anymore; we roared in on coffee fumes. So our nerves were already strung raw when the welfare debate kicked off with draconian suggestions. Cancel cash welfare to single mothers! Cancel payments to their children! "I'm waiting for the Speaker to say he's canceling Christmas," Lynn said. The strategy was an old one: Start off as severe as possible because the final result inevitably would be watered down. Then the Speaker held a press conference. I caught only smatterings, since the television set in the office was turned low, but I did hear the Speaker say, "I suggest everyone watch an excellent movie about this, *Boys Town*, with Spencer Tracy." I leaned back in my seat as my phone rang.

"Did I just hear the Speaker of the House refer to a movie to make a legislative point?" Lynn asked. "Did Robert write that?"

Robert was, after all, the guy who gleefully had pointed at the House chamber and exclaimed to a newspaper reporter, "The Zeitgeist starts here!"

I punched Robert's number. His voice was low and muffled. "Oh, well, the Speaker, the Speaker is talking about using orphanages to take care of children whose parents can't take care of them."

"Doesn't that already happen?" I asked.

"Well, yes, but this would be part of welfare reform." Robert paused. "I've got to go. I'll tell you more later."

But Lynn beat him to it. She showed up at my desk, her hands trembling as she clutched a sheaf of papers. "I think I'm about to break out in hives, " she announced. "Have you heard about this yet? Have you seen the Republican ideas? Do you know what they do? They take kids away from mothers on welfare and put them in orphanages!" Whatever was left of Lynn's self-proclaimed bleeding liberal heart gushed.

"Forcibly taking kids or is this a volunteer thing?" I asked.

"They don't say—what a surprise, when they're using a movie as a reference source!" she snapped. "You know who's been in these welfare briefings? Bob. I've got a few questions for *him.*"

She stomped away. I considered calling Bob to warn him, but why ruin the moment? Lynn found him on the escalators to the Capitol. She was going up; Bob was on the opposite side, going down.

"Taking kids away from their mothers because their mothers are poor!" she shouted at him. Even members stopped and stared. "So only rich people can have kids now?"

"Welfare needs to be reformed and you know it!" Bob yelled back.

"You're a coward. It's the smallest entitlement of all!" Lynn got the last word before they both disappeared into different hallways.

Welfare was only 3 percent of all entitlements, and the only part that didn't wholly affect the elderly. Joe Morgan insisted, "They were the boys and girls who saved the world." Maybe so, but they didn't do quite so well with their own country after the war. They went swinging through the subsidies—first with the federal school lunch program (created by Harry Truman when so many of them showed up at boot camp with rickets), then with the G.I. Bill and government housing loans for veterans. Meanwhile, over 40 percent of *their* grandparents scraped through on watery diets of flabby vegetables and canned meats. Once the "boys and girls who saved the world" became grandparents themselves, they turned a blind eye to the 25 percent poverty rate for their grandchildren. They cashed their Social Security checks and collected their Medicare coverage and made sure politicians knew they didn't want a single cent cut from their cherished programs. They conveniently dismissed the fact that if nothing was done, all of the national budget would be spent on the elderly by the early twenty-first century. Dan Rostenkowski tried to untangle the skein in 1983. Outraged seniors surrounded his car and rocked it until it nearly turned over.

Since some budget tinkering had to happen, Congress took on the one program that just happened to affect a constituency that never voted: children. I thought the orphanage reference looked mean. When I ran into Bob in the basement halls of Rayburn, I told him so. "Whatever," he said, shrugging; then, all aglow, "I just got out of a meeting with Newt. He had it for all the welfare legislative aides and legislative directors. And he told us that what we're doing is right, no matter what anyone says. We're *right*. Illegitimate births will go down, teenagers won't think about becoming mothers—"

"How many of them do you think get pregnant on purpose?" I asked.

"Come on." Bob smiled. "We know a lot of them do. And what we're doing will help them to stop."

"Orphanages will keep them from becoming pregnant," I repeated.

"Exactly."

I shook my head. "That's the stupidest thing I've ever heard."

Bob shrugged. "You're just mad," he said. "Lynn is, too. But you'll come around."

Come around! What was I on—the dark side? I glared at Bob, his face twisted into an expression of such condescension that my mind snapped. That was when I hit him—and nearly broke my hand in the process—and Bob just grinned, all his teeth flashing.

"You'll see," he said loftily.

"Oh, go to hell." I rubbed my hand and stormed away.

We made one more stab at civility when Bob, Lynn, and I met at Bardo's. We were exhausted emotionally before we even sat down, and after Lynn threw her drink at Bob none of us were talking to anyone not of our party. We weren't the only staffers affected. Interparty goodwill all but disappeared. Joe Morgan practically danced with glee. "I told you this would happen," he said to anyone within earshot. And so it seemed that 18–35 staffers weren't different at all from older Washingtonians. However our peers registered or voted or otherwise identified themselves, Hill staffers had the closest proximity to political power. If there really was an independent movement, we would have to buy into it, too—once we didn't swallow the establishment, where did that leave them? No wonder people like Joe Morgan began to breathe easier. They were practically incapable of understanding anything outside their way—the one that had brought so many "gate" scandals, trivial squabbles, and relentless finger-pointing. It was all they knew. So, thought the Joe Morgans, thank God the new crop was finally getting with the program!

But then, the establishment tripped. The House created block grants, lump sums that would be sent to the states and used at the states' discretion. Nutrition programs, which hadn't fallen under "welfare" before, were included in this: food programs for the elderly like Meals on Wheels and dinners at senior citizens' centers, and school lunches for children. As Dan Rostenkowski might have warned his former colleagues, touch any money for seniors and risk igniting the hellfires of the senior lobby. The elderly flooded Congress with letters and phone calls. Bob sifted through the stacks and piles of notecards and envelopes that faced him one morning: "Cut the kids! Keep our money federal!" He shook his head in disbelief.

"We need to have the federal government pay for meals at senior citizens' centers," a seventy-year-old woman told him. "It's our only place to socialize."

Bob tucked his face away from the receiver long enough to make a retching sound.

It wasn't happening just to Republicans. Lynn saw seniors corner Democratic members in the halls.

"Now you listen to me," an elderly woman said, crooking her finger at a miserable-looking congressman. "Those parents can pack a lunch. I did for my kids. They don't need the federal government paying for school lunches."

On and on and on. The complaints became so nightmarish ("I am sick and tired of seniors being treated this way! I paid my taxes and I want my meals at my center!") that we actually began to examine each other again, our eyes red-rimmed, empathy beginning to swell. And then it was the political establishment that gave the final push.

"Hey," Lynn said over the phone, her voice hoarse. "They cut a deal. School lunches are going into the block grants. All the senior stuff is staying federal. They got their fire wall."

There was no guarantee that any of the block grant money would be spent on school lunches. The governor of Mississippi had already announced that he couldn't promise anything.

"If you cut subsidies for school lunches, the schools are going to raise the price and that'll blackball even more kids from having meals." Lynn's voice got higher with each word.

I cleared my throat. "Who was it?" I asked. "The Republicans?"

She laughed bitterly. "I wish it was just them. The Democrats were in on it, too."

None of us should have been surprised. When *hadn't* both parties failed us equally? The one time that young aides abandoned caution and actually committed to a party, *and look what happened.* We choked on our indignation. But on the House floor, our bosses delivered their scripted parts.

"Good-bye, milk! Hello, Kool-Aid!" shouted a Democrat from North Dakota. "I wonder how many of my colleagues would like a diet like that for themselves?" Others threw on ties spotted with the faces of smiling children. To the credit of the Congress, not all members were so hypocritical. A large number witnessed the posturing with dismay. These were the men and women who genuinely worked hard at their jobs, infusing the office with honesty and dignity. Unfortunately, these members were never the ones in front of the cameras. And anyway, no matter how it was sliced, it was still the selling out of children who couldn't vote for older people who could, all glossed over with partisan rhetoric to save face.

I turned off the television, practically shaking as I walked out of the office, around a corner, and straight into Robert. He took one look at me and asked, "What happened to you?"

I clenched my jaw. "I'm out of here," I announced. This was it, my "come-to-Jesus" moment, and I wasn't sticking around. I didn't have the stomach to watch anymore.

"Well," Robert took this in stride, "why don't we go out for a beer instead?"

One building away, Bob ran into Lynn at the vending machine in the Longworth basement. She leaned against the glowing colors, catatonically holding a Coke. Without a word, Bob pushed quarters into the slot and waited for a can to thud to the bottom. He turned to Lynn.

"I can't defend this," he said. "I won't even call it cowardice, because cowardice injects an ethical battle into it."

"I know," she said softly. "Every time I think we can do something good, we just make things worse."

All of a sudden, clean party lines weren't such a sure thing anymore. The young electorate had rejected them, and now so had their counterparts on Capitol Hill. The members remained blissfully ignorant. Joe Morgan and his buddies didn't. They saw as plain as day what was happening. "You're either going to have to get with the program around here," Joe warned us, "or you're going to have to get out."

*Open Commitment*

So after seemingly endless speculation about how 18–35s were going to vote in 1996, consultants and politicians figured that the key description of the largest potential voting-age block was "potential." Despite early polls showing enthusiasm and an eagerness to cast ballots, young people did not turn out nearly as well as expected. They made up approximately 21 percent of the total vote. Then again, the much-prized senior citizens amounted to less than 23 percent, and the candidates had targeted *them*. "Proportionately, *nobody* turned out," says Jefrey Pollock, vice president of Global Strategy Group, Inc. This much was undeniable. Less than 50 percent of total eligible voters went to the polls—the lowest percentage since 1924. "There were real warning signs all year long," says Dave Anderson of MTV News. "Interest in the Republican field was low. Interest in Clinton was low."

"There is no better indication," says Kimberly Schuld, "that this was a boring election."

All sorts of theories floated: The economy was too profitably cushy; the campaign was too dull; the candidates were too similar; a Clinton victory seemed to be a foregone conclusion. But, among constituencies, the youth vote could not be ignored because such a dismal percentage of eighteen- to twenty-four-year-olds (approximately 29 percent) turned out. Al Gore made sure of that at the Youth Ball. The vice president could point to the estimated 50 percent of eighteen- to twenty-four-year-olds who supported Clinton over the 34 percent who voted for Dole. "Then again," former Senator Warren Rudman points out, "Bob Dole came from a party strong on prayer in schools, against abortion, preaching what values young people should use."

And, the eighteen to thirty-five voting bloc fragmented. In a generation marked by its diversity, roughly 40 percent of twenty-five- to thirty-five-year-olds voted. They broke down haphazardly: 46 percent for Clinton, 36 percent for Dole, 18 percent for independent candidates. They also had the highest level of split-ticket voting of any other age group, and many reported to the exit pollers that they had not bothered to fill out the entire ballot—if they didn't believe in a particular race, instead of simply putting a random mark by a name, they abstained. "That was *not* a surprise," says Curtis Gans, executive director of the Center for the Study of the American Electorate. "That segment is unpredictable—not a sure vote for anyone."

To some politicians, like former Democratic Congressman Tim Penny and former Democratic Senator David Boren, this indicated a need to temper both parties. They held meetings with like-minded colleagues across the country. But Penny and Boren believed the parties could be changed from *within*. Most of the 60 percent of 18–35s who had no party affiliation did not claim such a faith. The Democrats and Republicans paid scant attention to this. But, especially after the 1996 election, the Libertarian Party examined it closely. Their presidential candidate, Harry Browne, went to the wedding of his wife's nephew in late November, where a twenty-two-year-old woman approached him. "I voted for you," she said, "and many of my friends did, too."

Browne stared at her. He had been forewarned by her parents that she was the liberal of the family. "Well," he said, "how did *that* happen?"

"We saw you on *Politically Incorrect*," she said. "We were all impressed with the way you took the ribbing. You stood for something and you weren't defensive about it."

The same thing happened in John Kasich's reelection as representative from the Twelfth District of Ohio. "He talks about why we need to balance the budget, he says how he's going to do it, and if someone challenges him on his points, he doesn't sound condescending or uptight," explained a twenty-three-year-old registered Democrat who voted for the House budget committee chairman.

"He backs up everything he says." And in Massachusetts, voters nearly agonized over the Senate race that pitted Republican William Weld against Democrat John Kerry. Both men were fiscally conservative and socially moderate. Both possessed an air of decency and dependability. "I hated having to vote in that race," said a twenty-five-year-old independent. "But what a race! I believed in both of the candidates, which was nice for a change."

The message got through to the Libertarian Party. It immediately reconfigured its strategy around the eighteen- to thirty-five-year-old vote. "There is no doubt in my mind," Browne says now, "that if we want to capture 30 percent of the general electorate, we need to focus our resources on them." In his campaign report to the Libertarian Party, Browne emphasized the need for "an organized program to set up Libertarian clubs on college campuses." The party, which operates on a $2 million annual budget, has allotted $500,000 for that alone.

But the independent streak does not trickle out with the latter half of this generation. More than 50 percent of twelve- to seventeen-year-olds consider themselves independent. Traditionally, children have identified with whatever party their parents belong to, and the majority of these parents lean slightly to the Republicans. "These kids are growing up in a time when they're exposed to a lot more of how the world works at a younger age," says Kimberly Schuld. "Pretty much the only thing they've heard about politics for the past four years is how it doesn't work. Neither major party has really done anything, so why subscribe to them?"

Just as important, an independent vote to 18–35s is not seen as a wasted vote. This is partly because of the element of invincibility that historically comes with being young and prompts them to take risks. But the 18–35s put their own stamp on it. If they were like any other generation, their willingness to "risk" their vote for Ross Perot in 1992 wouldn't have translated into support for independent candidates in 1996. Four years, according to conventional

*A NEW KIND OF PARTY ANIMAL*

wisdom, is enough to restrain the impulses of youth. Instead, support for independents increased during that time among this group. If the current major parties are viewed as not accomplishing anything, what, exactly, are young people "wasting" by voting for a third party? Ultimately, the 18–35s go with what they believe, not with what the political establishment considers viable.

The day before the 1996 election, Kim Alexander's mother asked her who she would vote for. Kim didn't want to choose the "lesser of two evils." If she swallowed her standards, she would be accepting mediocrity. She wanted her vote to count for *some*thing. Ross Perot had been saying that if he got 25 percent of the vote, the Republicans and Democrats would have to let the Reform Party in the next presidential debates. Kim didn't think Perot would get anywhere near 25 percent this time around, but she pulled the lever for him anyway. One small step to show that politics would not continue as usual.

———

The welfare battle changed everything. Whatever inclination young staffers had to follow their elders into firm partisanship was irrevocably shattered. All bets were off now. Never, never, never would we blindly believe something as banal as *party lines*. Not that the political establishment lost much sleep over this, although it should have. We were the political establishment of the future, and if we didn't buy into their parties, where was that going to leave them? They didn't so much as yawn.

Instead, Congress launched itself into the first Medicare debate—from '95 into '96—another possible eye-glazer except that it gave members something new to throttle each other with. Democrats accused Republicans of tossing the nation's elderly into the cold world of the uninsured (forget the fact that eighteen- to thirty-five-year-olds were the least insured age group but still paying Medicare taxes); the GOP charged the Democrats with launching a "Mediscare" campaign. The Republicans talked about "Medicare savings"; the Democrats preferred "Medicare cuts." The House Democrats rolled out a Trojan horse on the grounds near the Capitol rotunda, a symbol for the cameras that staffers privately deemed "weak." A twenty-six-year-old Democratic legislative director sniffed, "You would think they could come up with a better sales pitch. Bor-ing." In return, the House Republicans trotted out an ostrich, to symbolize the Democrats sticking their heads into the ground to avoid reality, which staffers privately deemed "stupid." These were the first of many press stunts, all supposedly designed to "enlighten" the public. Young aides shook their heads. "I can't believe," Bob said, "that we're spending our time on this instead of real stuff."

And then, during the debate itself, Democrat Jim Moran from Virginia broke the finger of Randy "Duke" Cunningham, a Republican from California, in a fight just off the House floor while members like Bob Dornan ran around shouting, "No one tell the press! No one tell the press!" And of course, someone did. While our bosses railed to the C-Span cameras, Bob nearly collided with Lynn as he walked into an elevator.

"Have you seen this?" He held out a paper, his face a tight line of disgust. Lynn skimmed over the columns. It seemed Medicare wasn't going broke in 2002, like our bosses on both sides of the aisle were telling people. The hospital trust fund, which was part of Medicare, was out of money in *1996*. The Medicare "trust fund" itself would be tapped out by 2002 and become a pay-as-you-go system like Social Security.

"Do they know about this?" Lynn asked, astonished.

"Of course they do!" Bob snapped. "But instead of cooperating to get anything done, they're arguing about what words to use! They're just going to let this slide until they can do the easiest

*A NEW KIND OF PARTY ANIMAL*

thing, which is raise the payroll tax on everyone. We're screwed and everybody knows it. I wish they'd quit lying to us and let us plan."

Besides, seniors bought the "Mediscare" campaign. They stormed Capitol Hill, invading a Ways and Means Committee hearing on Medicare. Some had tied gags around their mouths. Others shouted, "We have no vote!" Bob, who was there, could scarcely believe this.

"All we've ever heard from them is how they *are* the vote!" he exclaimed. "What *is* it with these people?"

Interparty buzzing promptly returned to the staffer ranks like never before. We believed in this, and we were in a position to act on it even if our bosses couldn't get over their parties long enough to see straight. We exchanged memos and faxed facts. If the Joe Morgans of the Hill had thought we were disloyal before, we were downright mutinous now. Old standbys like, "Did you hear the one about the Republican who thought Huey Newton was a cookie?" were met with annoyance. Joe Morgan's partisan blusters were greeted with bemused stares. He could hardly believe his eyes: hundreds of young staffers boasting about supporting independent candidates, talking across party lines, and giving out *information.* I was sure that Jack Daniel's bottle in the bottom of Joe's lower-left desk drawer was quickly drained.

But, by the time Medicare reform collapsed under tiffs and spats, and after the intrepid national political reporters "suddenly" discovered that Medicare would go bankrupt six years ahead of schedule (touching off a finger-pointing debate between parties as to which one had lied about what), Joe Morgan gave up.

He handed in his resignation and left the Hill, the place he had always planned on spending his entire career. Joe Morgan had experienced a second "come-to-Jesus" moment, and this one he did not survive. "I just don't get this place anymore," Joe muttered.

*Open Commitment*

In 1996, the Democrats would structure their campaign strategies on the congressional and presidential levels around the heartless Republican plan to "cut Medicare." Clinton, especially, went after this, hard. By 1997, the Republican members of the House were shy about proposing any new Medicare measures, all problems with the program aside. A vicious pounding can have that effect. But when the Senate passed a bill that would increase Medicare co-payments for the wealthy and gradually raise the age of eligibility, Clinton vowed that he "would be happy to defend the vote of any member of Congress, Democrat or Republican" who supported the bill. "My best judgment [is] that a big majority of the American people will support this," Clinton said after meeting with his budget negotiators at the White House. "They understand how big the baby boomer retirement generation is." Republicans feared a trick, that they were being set up for another election-year bashing (the hopes of congressional Democrats to take back the majority in 1998 were hardly a secret), and the liberal Democrats grumbled cynically that this was an attempt by Clinton "to assure his place in history." But, the fact remained that *the subject had come up . . . again.* It wasn't going away. So let the Joe Morgans leave. Out with the old! In with the new!

But back in 1995, when the seeds of this had just begun to sprout, I walked across the Capitol grounds one evening, heading to the office. I understood the place. I was staying. So was Lynn, and Bob, too. But even if the Joe Morgans were losing ground, I couldn't gloat or grin about that yet. There was still a nagging voice inside, saying: *It's not enough, not enough, not enough.* I couldn't shake it or figure it out. Then, someone cleared his throat. It was Robert, standing on the vast lawn littered with fresh grass clippings. "Hi," he said quietly. He looked past me at the House chamber. The dome lit up under a sky bleeding pink in the setting sun.

"Thinking about Zeitgeist again?" I teased. Robert allowed himself a small smile.

"Actually, chess," he said. "Add it all up, and that's what we're playing."

He glanced again at the dome and then back at me. "Endgame," he said, "is here."

# Chapter Three

# *BLOCK BY BLOCK*

*In the past two decades, American priorities have shifted away from promoting the well-being of children and toward promoting the well-being of adults.*

—Norval Glenn,
sociologist,
University of Texas

Quillie Coath Jr. cradled the phone in his neck. "That's a buncha crap because it's politics!" He gestured expansively. "There's a buncha money going to people without kids!" Endgame. Yeah, Quillie would agree with that. Robert George might be thinking about this on Capitol Hill, but 400 miles south, where the roads gashed through swaths of piney green and the air hung hot and heavy ("Ever been inside a dryer?" Quillie once asked), Quillie could hear the minutes ticking away, too.

Usually, Quillie didn't have time to breathe, let alone figure out the broad scheme of things. His friends only half-jokingly referred to him as "the Man," because when it came to juvenile intervention, Quillie really *was* the Man. Durham, North Carolina, didn't crackle with crime like most larger cities, but it had its problems all the same. Growing up, Quillie had a close view as a slew of kids in his neighborhood slid into the gooey muck of the system—the schools, the courts, the jails. If you messed up once, it was like stepping through a rotted floorboard, because chances were, you fell all the way down. Quillie himself didn't have an opportunity to screw up. His teachers from elementary school through high school had not only taught his two older brothers, they had also had his parents, his aunts, and his uncles in their classes. By the time Quillie came through, oh, they were ready for *him*. There was someone's foot on his back the whole way, holding him accountable and kicking him toward success.

If Quillie's friend Jeff had gotten this treatment, he might have made it. Jeff went to school with Quillie—he was practically a genius, hacking and tapping away on computers long before anyone else in his class. But Jeff, with all his brains, ended up in jail and drank until his liver withered yellow. Some people might have chalked this up to the single-parent-household syndrome. But Jeff's mother had turned out two older sons just fine, with or without their father being around. What Jeff didn't need, in Quillie's opinion, was any of this psychoanalysis crap: What drove you to this? How do you feel? No one asked Quillie how he *felt* when he goofed off in ninth grade and got in-school suspension as a result. When the principal called his mother, she refused point-blank to pick up her son. "You got yourself into trouble," she said, "so you can just stay there." Quillie had to call his uncle, a police officer, to come get him. The wrath of a policeman was nothing to what his mother was going to do to him. *How do you feel, Quillie? I feel* stupid, *thanks.* He was well aware of what his

A NEW KIND OF PARTY ANIMAL

mother would say: that any son of hers knew right from wrong.

Quillie looked like a political consultant's dream. His face cut between easygoing lines and intense sternness. Depending on the moment, his thin mustache seemed either dashing or paternal—not much of a surprise, since he was a single father. And not only was he tall and strapping, Quillie also gushed with such charisma that he could sell ice cubes to an Eskimo. He didn't want to run for office, though. He was too busy running the P.R.O.U.D. (Personal Responsibility to Overcome with Understanding and Determination) Program, serving on the board of directors for the Wake County Council for Adolescent Pregnancy and as an advisory board participant for the Save Our Students Program at Carnage Middle School in Wake County, volunteering as a male responsibility trainer for the Durham County Health Department, and as a facilitator for the Domestic Violence Program of Wake County. He wasn't doing it for the money, that was for sure. And for the skeptics who thought it as just so *cute* that he worked in community-based nonprofit, well, that was the game these days. Changes didn't come in sweeps. Changes came block by block. You could *see* results, not just read about them through polls or studies. Start with so many blocks and soon you have a neighborhood, then a city, then a county, and on and on. Since mistrust of government ran strong and deep among 18–35s, it was only natural that activism on the local level would appeal to them. A survey of college freshmen by UCLA's Higher Education Research Institute, which began in the 1960s, found that in 1997 about 72 percent of students said they had performed volunteer work in the past year, the highest the study has ever recorded. Even if they weren't waving placards, like the boomers had done thirty years before, young people were politically active—in concrete, local ways.

So when Quillie decided to tackle troubled youth, he knew he had to do it from the ground up. When the word on the streets declared probation to be "cool," and when playing dumb in class was "hip," Quillie knew he had to get to the individual to make a difference. The P.R.O.U.D. Program took eight young people, between thirteen and seventeen, and for twelve weeks put them through weekly meetings, community service, and field trips to jails and courts. They ended up in the program for various reasons—everything from assault to possession of weapons. P.R.O.U.D. was their alternative to juvenile hall. It worked, because Quillie was good at it and a natural. "The best," said Charles McKinney, who sat just down the hall in the cramped office where the air conditioner dripped into the plaster walls as he furiously punched phone numbers. In a suit, Charles looked like an investment banker. In jeans, he looked like an investment banker on vacation. His appearance outlined his life: the affable grin that cracked across his face came from his California upbringing; the scrutinizing glance behind gold-rimmed glasses came from Morehouse College; and the shaved head came as a result of his receding hairline, which came courtesy of the stress of graduate school at Duke. Charles ran the Durham Service Corps' summer jobs program for fifty teens between sixteen and twenty; good, solid experience beyond flipping burgers, which was what most of these lower-to-middle-class kids would otherwise land.

Only a year apart—Quillie was twenty-seven, Charles twenty-eight—they pretty much exhaled confidence as they strode together down the halls of the old elementary school purchased by the Durham Service Corps. This was something new to the teens who ended up in front of their desks. Baggy jeans, backward baseball caps, faces smeary with nonchalance as they viewed the world through slitted eyes—Quillie and Charles wanted to shake every last one out of their undereducated, underemployed existence and kick their butts into the twenty-first century before they were eaten alive. Because if they didn't get it with Quillie or Charles, they wouldn't get it at all.

Programs like theirs scare people today, who want more jails, tougher penalties. Anyone under fifteen is seen as a scourge waiting to happen. In a move that boiled Quillie's temper, North Carolina lowered the age to qualify for trial as a legal adult from sixteen to thirteen. Quillie was not given to many words—he made his points quickly and succinctly. "Ever since they came out with the name 'Generation X,'" he said, "I knew that everyone after that was just going to get crucified. 'X' is near the end of the alphabet. No one wants to deal with what's really going on, so they just label us as near the end, and the kids behind us . . ." Quillie trailed off. Because there was a new tag line: "Generation Y" ("Does this mean our kids'll be 'Z'?" Charles wondered). And even worse, "superpredators." Sociologists used it, politicians co-opted it, and journalists repeated it. These six-, seven-, eight-year-old children were declared by James Q. Wilson, a professor of public policy at UCLA, to be "youngsters who . . . show us the blank, unremorseful stare of a feral, presocial being." What a change from 1989, when a federal judge had declared that Quillie's peers were unsavable and that society should focus instead upon "the younger group, concentrate on the kindergartners."

Quillie shook his head. "Crucified," he quietly repeated. He could tick off the real problems: lousy schools, disinterested parents, drugs. But who wanted to hear the truth when this seductive "superpredator" term existed? Quillie felt as if he were facing down a tidal wave. Over 700 pieces of legislation on the national and state levels were passed in 1995, increasing the penalties for minors ("These little turkeys have got total contempt for us, and it's time to do something," said New Hampshire State Representative Richard Kennedy on legislation he cosponsored that called for the public, bare-bottomed spankings of convicted teenage vandals). Two years later, Senator Orrin Hatch would attempt to push through the Judiciary Committee over 100 amendments that increased penalties for juvenile offenders saying, "People are expecting us to do something about these violent teenagers."

Hatch would help kick off yet another round of chicken between the president and Congress: Who could be more zealous about crime? "Crime," of course, meant "juvenile offenders." Blithely sidestepping the fact that 84 percent of the nation's counties had no juvenile homicides at all, the House of Representatives—purportedly responding to a scourge of young killers—would vote to offer states $1.5 billion in financial incentives to require that juveniles arrested for violent crimes be tried as adults. And, President Clinton would declare his top law-enforcement priority to be tougher penalties for any young offender. But they all missed the harsh truth that prisons are usually savage places. Countless stories attested to this. There was the fifteen-year-old girl in Ohio who ran away from home for one night and returned voluntarily, only to have a judge put her in jail to "teach her a lesson." The girl had never been in trouble before. Her fourth night behind bars, she was sexually assaulted by a guard. Or, there was the seventeen-year-old boy in Idaho who failed to pay $73 in traffic fines. He was jailed, and adult prisoners tortured and then killed him. Or, there was the sixteen-year-old Texas boy who was sentenced to eight years for an arson fire that did $500 worth of damage to a fence. Within two weeks, he was raped, and then attacked repeatedly until he hanged himself.

Still, the politicians persisted. They offered to build more jails. "Ah, the industry of the future," Charles said. He didn't bother to bite back the bitterness. Almost every major city in the country had built a new stadium and a new jail, and Durham went with the trend. A gleaming new stadium and then an imposing new jail rose up in concrete blocks. Every time he passed the jail, Charles's teeth ached. "Lock 'em up and deal with 'em later," he muttered. "That's all they can come up with."

Quillie and Charles had stacks of studies and evidence that showed children to be less likely to commit violent crime if they had a responsible adult in their lives. Parent, teacher, coach, counselor—it didn't matter who it was as long as someone gave guidance and attention. And this was old news. Theodore Roosevelt Sr., the father of the future president, knew this in 1869 when he started the Newsboys' Lodging House in New York City, where each night several hundred stray boys ("street rats," as the police called them) were given a clean bed in a warm room and daily visits from Roosevelt himself. A quarter of a century after his death in 1878, his son Teddy, then governor of New York, was with some of his colleagues at a conference when Joseph Brady, the governor of the Alaska Territory, made it a point to find him. Brady wanted to shake the hand of the son of the first Theodore Roosevelt, he said, because the first Theodore Roosevelt had made him who he was. Governor Brady had been picked off the streets as a boy by TR's father, who then put him in the Newsboys' Lodging House until he could place Brady in a home in the West. TR's father had paid for Brady's travel there, and had checked on his progress as he grew up.

Yes, Charles thought, the key was guidance and attention. But somewhere along the way, this responsibility had been shoved off. Well, Charles didn't have to believe what politicians or the media dished at him. He knew the truth. He was up to his elbows in it.

Just down the hall, Quillie listened sympathetically to the sad story of one of his P.R.O.U.D. kids. Charles had the routine down. Next, he would hear Quillie tell the boy firmly, "Regardless of what your parents did or didn't do, you know what's right and what's wrong. My mother used to tell me, 'You've got to be responsible for yourself, and that means you might have to stand alone. Don't go because the crowd says to. You need to know when to go home.'" He would pause for effect, then tell the child, "Sometimes I think that's the straightest thing I've ever heard."

———

It was the stuff that made political speechwriters salivate. In spring 1997, *The Washington Post* reported that a spindly twelve-year-old boy, living in a decaying neighborhood in the southeastern section of the nation's capital, surrounded by spray-painted war cries and memorials to the dead, fired a gun at a sixteen-year-old gang member. Darryl Dayan Hall wanted to be in a gang, too ("It's time for a new generation," he wrote in a three-ring notebook). But when Jovan "Tweety" James broke his leg, running away from Hall, he decided the kid needed a call. "You're too young for this," James said. He later claimed that Darryl Hall rebuffed the warning, so, James concluded, "I guess [he] wanted to die."

In January 1997, James and two fellow gang members (or, according to prosecutors, three) spotted Darryl Dayan Hall walking home from school, chased him a block before catching him, and threw him into a car. Hall was shot twice—once in the leg and then in the back of the head—and left dead, in a ditch. This sad, short story had all the pathos of stolen childhood and the ominous warning of a juvenile gone bad, favorite themes of the political establishment. Darryl Dayan Hall made for perfect fodder, just as eleven-year-old Yummy Sandifer had three years before, when he was executed (there is no other word for a kid who is driven to a railroad underpass in Chicago and shot twice in the back of the head) for accidentally shooting a fourteen-year-old girl instead of rival gang members. These urban nightmares click off with such regularity that politicians offer canned answers: "He slipped between the cracks"; "What kind of a future do our children have?"; "We must not let this happen again."

Yet their solutions, if politicians give up their partisan tiffs long enough to reach any, are always along the route of tougher sentencing or more jails. This despite a 1996 study by the RAND Corporation that found preventive measures to be more cost-effective than increasing prison terms in reducing crime, or the conclusion by John DiIulio Jr., a crime expert who teaches at

*A NEW KIND OF PARTY ANIMAL*

Princeton, that "Most kids who get into serious trouble with the law need adult guidance, and they won't find suitable role models in prison." Ah, but such a course of action would take the two things that not just politicians but older age groups as well find all but impossible to accept: time and personal involvement.

No wonder that instead of waiting for politicians to get their collective act together, most 18–35s took matters into their own hands—literally. They knew that the sweat of the brow worked. "We don't believe in wasting time, discussing how great it is that we're getting involved locally or dissecting theories," Heather McLeod says pointedly. The twenty-eight-year-old former editor of the community activism magazine *WhoCares* adds, "We can *see* the impact when we volunteer. We know the difference is real." Over 74 percent of 18–35s believe community involvement can make a genuine difference. To that end, young people offer up 2.1 billion hours of volunteer service each year in their neighborhoods, more than any other age group.

And, why wouldn't young people feel compelled to have a stake in their community? Very few had grown up in the Eisenhower-era ideal of the "nuclear family." Instead, they had come of age at a time when, every day, over 2,500 children witness the divorce or separation of their parents and 90 children are taken from their parents' custody and placed in foster homes. A majority of absentee parents in the 1980s and 1990s are a dozen times more likely to be up-to-date on their car payments than their child support payments. It's no surprise that 18–35s determinedly set about to do things differently. But, they take community activism further than its strict definition. They apply it to their votes.

"The activism is more sophisticated than ever," says twenty-six-year-old Therese Heliczer, executive director of the Center for Environmental Citizenship. "We as an age group directly tie our community work to our vote. We bring the issue we care about to the ballot box. No one's ever done that before."

Quillie and Charles did. During the 1996 campaign, they flipped on their television sets and there was the "new" image of Clinton as National Dad, sternly telling them from the election pulpit that school uniforms and curfews were the way to solve juvenile crime. School uniforms! Curfews! Quillie and Charles would have howled if it weren't so painful. School uniforms weren't going to help the kids walking through metal detectors. School uniforms weren't going to help the eleven-year-old in Chicago who attended the funeral of a classmate and said emotionlessly, "The only way to get out is to die." Or what about the psychiatric evaluation that Yummy Sandifer took, when the examiner asked Yummy to complete the sentence "I am very . . ." "Sick," Yummy replied. School uniforms, indeed. Just like Quillie said, it was crap because it was politics.

———

Charles heard the news about the welfare bill on his way to the Durham Service Corps. What a way to start the morning. "Congress has passed legislation that will give states more authority— and require welfare recipients to work," rolled the caramel-coated voice of the radio reporter. Charles snapped off the station. He thought the welfare bill was grounds for an aneurysm.

He didn't have to think about it. His ten-month stint with the Durham Service Corps was about over. He was getting married. Now *that* he thought about. And then he would be back in graduate school and working part-time at an organization called Public Allies, which placed people in nonprofit jobs. Charles would be in charge of finding employment for eight people and monitoring their progress. Eight people—that didn't sound like much, but it was a start. After all this up-close experience with the job market, Charles didn't have a problem with a hand up instead of a hand out—who did?—but why, he wondered, was it that whenever we wanted to start tightening our belts we started with the lowest rung? The question was rhetorical. Charles knew the answer.

It would have been easy to not even ask it. He grew up wrapped comfortably in middle-class trimmings, in cookie-cutter houses linked with ribbons of grass. His father was dean of admissions at UC Santa Barbara. His mother was a real estate agent. But there were always reminders that other people didn't live this way. The aunts and uncles he visited every summer—they qualified as working class. They didn't have eggs for breakfast, like Charles was used to. As a result, Charles developed a slight but steady streak of paranoia. "Yeah, we're cool now," he once told his father, "but what *if*. I mean, Dad, is everything *paid for?*"

When he went to Morehouse College, it would have been easy to keep his head down on the way to class. But the west end of Atlanta surrounded three sides of the campus: broken bottles, swollen bellies, ragtag kids. Charles took a hard look and asked himself the questions that would echo for years: What is your relationship with your community going to be? If you see it needs help, are you going to do your part? Charles didn't know how he couldn't get involved. He had read about poverty and crime. He had bantered about it in the dormitories. Now, he had to put his actions where his mouth was.

With nine friends, he started a fraternity based around community activism. "Kemet" meant "The Black Land" ("If you're going to have a fraternity at a black school, it shouldn't have a Greek name," Charles said). Kemet held book fairs and blood drives and organized tutorials between Morehouse students and neighborhood kids. Five years after Charles graduated, the fraternity would have over 150 members.

It would have been easy after this to travel or take a corporate job or any of the other usual options. Charles had a year before he would go to Duke to get his Ph.D. in history. But he became a teacher—in Compton, no less, one of the poorest sections of Los Angeles—by accident. He thought he was up for a job as an on-site coordinator for the district's Black Male Achievement Program. He sat in the principal's office and suddenly realized that she kept asking him questions about teaching.

"Um, excuse me, but what does teaching have to do with the Black Male Achievement Program?" Charles asked.

"Nothing," the principal replied. "I'm interviewing you for a teaching position."

"But I've never taught in my life!" Charles exclaimed. "I don't know anything about it!"

The principal looked at him sternly. "We *need* teachers."

Charles took the job. In the grip of that death stare, he had little choice. He moved in with an aunt in Inglewood, near the Forum, where the Lakers played and where police helicopters clattered through the night sky, beaming bright lights into suspicious corners. Two days after his interview, school started.

He had twenty-seven third-graders. Even now, driving through the sweltering streets of Durham, Charles could remember the day he asked his kids, "Has anyone ever seen or known anyone who's been shot?" Damn near every hand went up. Charles felt his heart sink. Oh God, he thought as he looked out at the sea of small palms, why are you being subjected to this?

"Mr. McKinney, Mr. McKinney!" one boy frantically waved. "I know a kid, he got shot in the head. The bullet went in, and then smoke came out, and then blood came out, and then he fell over."

Charles stared, horrified. This kid was eight years old and he could give, in detail, what happened to the human body when it got shot. This was happening all over, and not just to children in ghettos. Charles had gone to the Durham Service Corps with the numbers ringing in his ears: Nationally, across the economic spectrum, one in six kids between ten and seventeen had seen or knew someone who had been shot; children were 244 percent more likely to be killed by guns now than they were in 1986. That was nasty, Charles thought, that was pathetic. The whole violence issue was a confluence of all the other issues that he dealt with, primarily education and employment.

Ah, yes, education. Man, if there was another subject guaranteed to get him going, it was the deplorable state of public education in the country. Charles had watched as the two guys who ran that Lead or Leave group thrust themselves into the white-hot media spotlight by bashing the national debt. Charles didn't disagree that the debt was a problem, he just tied it to issues that affected his community. He wasn't stupid. He knew it was the domino effect—knock one down, the other would fall, too. Because of the debt and the deficit and the enormous chunks of the budget that were spent on the elderly, other programs (somewhat suspectly labeled "discretionary") lost out. Since kids didn't vote, and with young people considered ill-mannered at best and superpredators at worst, the powers-that-be had very few qualms about whittling away at education. If termites burrow long enough and deep enough, chewing until the hardest wood softens and splits into splinters and pits, even a tree that has withstood everything else that nature and man can throw at it will fall. A veteran schoolteacher told a researcher in 1983 about longing for the days of the 1950s—not because the children behaved better or because they were smarter. "We couldn't have had a more supportive community," the teacher said. "We never had a bond issue that was voted down. Anything the school wanted, we could get." In 1955, two-thirds of Americans were willing to pay extra taxes for schools. Good thing all those shiny, cinderblock schools were built in the fifties, because less than thirty years later adults would completely reverse this sentiment. Only 30 percent of Americans said they were willing to pay more for schools. Throughout the 1970s, just four dollars were approved by voters for every ten requested by school boards. And then, in 1978, California voters would pass a measure that would have a devastating effect on the state's public schools for the next twenty years.

It was called Proposition 13, and it slashed property taxes—which was California's primary source of funding for schools—by more than half. Thirty-seven other states would follow with similar legislation over the next two years. By the time the bloodletting ceased, the damage had been complete and ruthless. By 1983, an estimated $25 billion in repairs were needed in schools nationwide. A survey of 100 school districts in 34 states found that 71 percent of the schools needed roof repairs or even replacements, 25 percent needed new heating or air-conditioner equipment, and one in five buildings failed fire and safety standards. And amid the flaking asbestos, water-stained walls, curling paint, torn carpeting, outdated books, and rusting lockers, 18–35s grew up. "For the first time in the history of our country," proclaimed a 1983 report by the National Commission on Excellence in Education, "the educational skills of one generation will not surpass, will not equal, will not even approach, those of their parents." Well, Charles could tell them where to stick their damn report. Where the hell did they get off, slicing and dicing education like an onion, and then somehow expect kids to *learn?* His peers had pulled it off, though. Despite the long odds predicted by the commission's report, more 18–35s went to college than any generation before them. But then, deep inside, Charles thought most of his peers knew that they would escape the public elementary and high schools before the worst days arrived. Why else would they enter the notoriously underpaid and overworked profession of teaching in such numbers, the likes of which were wholly unexpected. Charles might have wandered into teaching by accident, but thank God he did. He could do something about the flailing system, even if it was for just a handful of kids. If the adults of this country wouldn't do the right thing, then Charles's age group was determined to.

His twenty-seven-year-old counterpart over at the North Carolina Employment Security Commission, Darryl Hedgepeth, once told Charles about the time he lived with his grandmother, eating ketchup and mustard sandwiches while his parents worked desperately to finish school and land decent jobs. "I did crazy stuff," Darryl said. "My parents were always working. I just knew I was going to hell or to jail. Then my grandmother started telling me about my grandfather, Ogala. Can you imagine being named Ogala? You'd think people'd mess with him, with a name like that. *Nobody* messed with him. He stood six four, darker than slate. A real bad boy. My grandmother told me stories, and I thought, well, I've got to get it together. I had to join the navy to do that, but it worked. So I know for a fact: People's lives are at stake out there. I know this firsthand."

Charles's anger crept up his neck and into his eyes, until he practically saw red. So the politicians thought they had solved welfare. Well, Charles hadn't heard them asking themselves the tough questions—and in this, Charles wasn't demanding that they do anything that he hadn't done as well. He knew what he'd fire at them: What are the sources of youth crime? Why are young people criminals? Why are young people so highly unemployable? Why is the public school system failing kids? What are the options we have? How can we work together to solve this? You say that parents need to get involved—well, mom works eleven hours a day; when is she going to get *involved?* You say you want to get government off our backs so we can take care of the problem—take care *how?* These were the hard questions that Charles wanted to hear, and if he was the one who got to ask them, you could bet those politicians weren't going to squirm away with sugar-coated, say-nothing sound bites. No way—Charles would *nail* those bastards.

He worked this through in his mind, raging silently as he walked up to the brick building. Melancholy cypress and juniper trees had pushed up sidewalks with their bulbous roots. Now the

*Block by Block*

concrete, once so solid, looked like broken pieces of candy. Charles rattled his office keys in the lock, and as the knob turned, it came to him. His third-graders would be in the tenth grade right now. Charles sat at the battered wooden desk and stared at the saxophone poster on the wall across from him. His little guys were in the tenth grade. He switched on his computer and wondered how many of them had actually made it that far.

———

It was called the Presidents' Summit for America's Future. Bill and Hillary Clinton; Al and Tipper Gore; all the living ex-presidents (Nancy Reagan represented her husband); thirty governors; ninety mayors; and one former chairman of the joint chiefs of staff came together at the end of April 1997 in the City of Brotherly Love, no less, to tout volunteerism as the way to save "young people who are disengaged from American life, who don't believe in the American dream." That was how Colin Powell, who chaired the summit, put it.

They wanted to encourage more Americans to volunteer. "It's about service, the future, and our children's well-being," said George Bush. And it all made for a lovely photo opportunity— even the event's staffers privately admitted that ("It was amazing how interested Clinton and everyone else got when they saw how much attention the summit was getting," said one). But, it was soaked in condescension. Here young people had been volunteering in record numbers for years, *on their own*, because they felt compelled to do so. And when acknowledgment of that finally arrived, what happened? Their elders didn't say things like, "Good for you for taking the lead!" or, "What can we learn from you?" Instead, they swept in as if to announce that the calvary had finally arrived. They were ready to take charge. "It's good to have an army again!" Powell cried, saluting a cheering crowd.

*A NEW KIND OF PARTY ANIMAL*

Maybe these leaders truly believe in community service—Powell also launched a group called America's Promise: The Alliance for Youth—but they came late to the battle. The 18–35s were already there. They did not need a pep rally to make them aware of the approximately 15 million children who are growing up in poverty. And most 18–35s recognized the summit for what is was: a *symbol*. The speeches and the posturing were about providing images, a technique that Clinton and his cohorts had perfected from their placard days.

But since 18–35s don't deal in tokens, many scrutinized Clinton's call for mandatory community service in order to graduate from high school. The state of Maryland already has this. So do many school districts throughout the country. Long before older Americans came up with the idea that volunteerism should be *required* (something that in itself is ironic), young people were involved in their communities. And, they saw this brainstorm as turning the concept of volunteering to help others into volunteering to help themselves. "The disappearance of the principle behind volunteering is a sad testament to the narcissistic nature of our society," wrote one high-schooler in a letter to *The New York Times*.

A high school student in Bethlehem, Pennsylvania, who on her own gave hundreds of hours as a Meals on Wheels aide and as a Girl Scout, challenged the notion of mandatory volunteerism in court. She lost. "As graduation neared, a school official pulled me aside and said it was not too late to change my mind," she said. "'After all,' he said, 'what is more important, your values or your diploma?'" Even though the student had continued volunteering, she did not submit her hours for credit. Instead of a diploma, she eventually earned a graduate equivalency degree.

"Volunteering is not about making yourself feel good," says Charles McKinney. "You do it because you want to really see a difference." That is what separates the brand of activism practiced by

18–35s from that of older Americans. Media coverage of the presidents' summit pointed out other spurts of civic duty that had eventually fallen away: a playground in Philadelphia built by volunteers five years before that hadn't been maintained and is now used as a market by drug dealers; graffiti-covered walls in Chicago that had been painted, only to be scrawled over completely less than a year later. These are cosmetic changes. The brand of community activism that Charles McKinney and Quillie Coath talk about is sustained, one-on-one contact, the hardest of all to keep up but the only kind that has proved to work.

Four days after the summit, columnist William Raspberry proclaimed, "I see nothing but good coming from this undertaking." Charles thought about this a moment.

"Well," he said, "let's see who sticks around. I know who I'm betting on."

———

In Durham, if the school district thought a kid was a problem, they put him in Halloway Street School. Nearly every school district in the country had a badass school, as Quillie called them. The problem was, a lot of the kids who ended up at Halloway weren't badasses. Sure they had problems, but what teenager didn't? Halloway slapped on a label that was hard to tear off. If you went to a school where the entire student body was trying to be tough, you were going to have a rough time assimilating back into a "regular school." Just the past week, a fifteen-year-old Halloway boy had slumped in front of Quillie, his pants hanging down and his cap backward. He'd been labeled with a third-grade reading level by virtue of his test scores, and sent to Halloway.

"Are you a dummy?" Quillie asked him.

"I ain't no dummy."

"Well, this test says you are." Quillie waved it in front of him.

*A NEW KIND OF PARTY ANIMAL*

No one had bothered to explain this before, what exactly the test meant. The kid took it again, this time with effort. He tested at a college reading level.

Quillie saw lots of kids like this—black, white, boy, girl. Those specifics didn't matter. If they messed up in the second grade, they got classified as underachievers and worse. And if they didn't have parents who went down to the schools to raise holy hell, the kids stayed there. Quillie had seen kids labeled "learning disabled" because they didn't know the word "skillet." He didn't know why that would be a surprise, when 36 percent of kids today fixed their own meals, mostly by popping frozen food in a microwave oven. Even worse, at the first sign of trouble, many parents dismissed any discussion and tried to put their children on Ritalin or Prozac. In some classrooms nationwide, 20 to 30 percent of students took the drugs.

Quillie had other ways. He worked very hard developing his ideas, picking them apart, and implementing them. If a concept didn't work, he got rid of it. He didn't have time to wait. Crime prevention was filled with soft-bellied theories that bureaucrats clung to even after the core had rotted away.

"The Mind *Is* and Always Will Be Our Primary Business." Quillie tacked this, bulletin-board style, on the wall in his office. Today marked graduation for his first P.R.O.U.D. class. He knew that most of them would leave acting big and bad, like they didn't know anything. They had learned. And inevitably, a few would trickle back to Quillie to tell him. For now, Quillie planned the graduation ceremony. The judge who had sentenced the boys would be there. So would the district attorney and the boys' families. He left the final discussion class to Charles to teach.

Six of the eight class members were there. Four sat around a table and two sprawled on a couch. "How was your week?" Charles began congenially.

"Worrisome," said a fourteen-year-old with enormous, thick

*Block by Block*

glasses. He was helping to coach an elementary school basketball team. "The children get on my nerves. I yell at them and they still won't be quiet."

The rest of the boys remained silent.

"So absolutely nothing happened with the rest of you?" Charles prodded. "Steven?"

Steven, a thick sixteen-year-old, looked at Charles. "I slept. Went outside. Sat down."

"So you pretty much sit down seven days a week and then come here?" Charles laughed. "That's quite an existence."

Silence.

"Well, this is your very last class," Charles said. "Then you graduate. We're going to have Judge Whaley there—" This elicited a chorus of boos. "What me and Quillie want to know is, do you guys have any idea who you want to come speak?"

"Michael Jordan!" shouted fifteen-year-old James, roused from his slump on the sagging couch.

"Okay. I'll put in a call." Charles grinned. "How 'bout this? How 'bout some guys from Durham?"

"Halle Berry!" cried Steven. All six faces lit up.

"Halle Berry's not from Durham." All six faces fell.

Charles passed out pencils. "I want you to write down some suggested speakers, and we'll see if we can get them. Now, here's my question: Why are you in this program?"

"To stay outta trouble," muttered Patrick, a giant of a sixteen-year-old.

Charles shook his head. "Don't give me the canned answer."

"My probation officer told me I had to come?" tried Steven.

"The actions I did," said a grim fourteen-year-old. "The repercussions were big."

"Let me tell you something," Charles said. "A friend of mine works in the D.A.'s office in New York. He told me that if you owe a drug dealer money, he shoots you in the back. In the old days, two years ago, he'd just shoot you. Now, it's a matter of getting paralyzed."

"But that's those guys. That's *them*," James insisted.

"That's right. That's them. You've learned to stay away from that crap. But, fifteen years ago, a drug dealer never would've shot you—he would've cut you. Fifteen years before that, he would've beat you up. Stuff changes. Actions have consequences. Forever. The second bit of information you need to know: You don't even *have* to do anything wrong. You just have to be next to the man next to the man next to the man who's doing the shit.

"The reason we tell you this every week is because young people are so damn hardheaded. If you'd listened to someone, you wouldn't be here right now. That's why me and Quillie keep telling you don't do this, don't do that. So, fellas, don't front. Some of you didn't have another option than coming here."

Quillie watched from the doorway. This was the reality behind the "crime issue." This was what he thought about when he headed to the polling booths every election cycle, not commercials or campaign slogans or "packaging." Quillie concerned himself with only gritty bits of fact. One day soon, he thought, and sooner than anybody ever imagined, politics would have to get real. It wasn't healthy to be fed a steady diet of crap. *Answer this question, Yummy: "I am very . . . " "Sick."*

Quillie looked long and hard at his P.R.O.U.D. kids and thought it was a real shame that one of them couldn't go to a White House press conference. If politicians thought they had to answer tough inquiries from reporters now, wait until a fifteen-year-old kid got hold of them.

## Chapter Four

# *THE SELLING OF THE PRESS-IDENT*

**spin** (spin) *vt.* **spun** or archaic **span, spun, spin'ning** [ME. *spinnen*< OE *spinnan*, akin to G. *spinnen* < IE. base *(s)pen(d)-, to pull, draw, spin] **1.** *a)* to draw out and twist fibers into thread *b)* to make by this process **2.** to make (a web, etc.) from a filament of a viscous fluid that is extruded from the body and hardens on exposure to the air; said of spiders, etc. **3.** to make or produce in a way suggestive of spinning

—Webster's Ninth New Collegiate Dictionary

Three weeks after Quillie and Charles watched the first P.R.O.U.D. kids graduate, the quadrennial party conventions began. Once, presidential candidates were actually chosen at these. In the original smoke-filled rooms, potential nominees cut deals in the scramble for delegates. Whoever had a majority by the time they hit the convention floor won, although sometimes not even then. At the 1952 Republican convention, Senator Everett Dirksen (who was supporting Robert Taft for president) railed from the podium at former presidential candidate Thomas Dewey (who was supporting Dwight Eisenhower), "We followed you before and you took us down the road to defeat!" Adlai Stevenson threw open a multi-ballot battle between John Kennedy, Estes Kefauver, and Albert Gore Sr., when he couldn't decide on a running mate in 1956. But midway through the twentieth century, this changed. The candidates almost always had been finalized before the conventions even opened. The conventions became the ultimate political commercials. Seasoned reporters like columnist Jeff Greenfield plainly longed for the good ol' days. "Think of an aging musician stopping on a street corner where a great dance palace once stood, yearning for one more Big Band night, when men in white dinner jackets pressed golden horns to their lips while a woman in a red evening gown and a flower in her hair sang plaintively of love," Greenfield wrote in *Time* magazine. There wasn't much use anymore for white dinner jackets in an era of casual Fridays.

In 1996, with Clinton's generation firmly in charge, symbolism took on a distinctly new twist. George Bush's peers used universal symbols to make their points. How did we know George Bush was patriotic? He visited a flag factory during the 1988 campaign. How did we know Ronald Reagan believed in freedom and the individual? He wore a cowboy hat and rode a horse. Clinton's peers used personal testimony. How did we know Clinton was against drugs? He discussed the addictions of his brother. How did we know Vice President Gore was opposed to cigarettes? He testified about the death of his sister from lung cancer, vowing to work "until my last breath" against tobacco marketing to children (he · neglected to include the fact that he had continued to raise and sell tobacco on his farm in Tennessee for several years after her death, even bragging about this in a speech to tobacco farmers in 1988). In this political world, as Robert George pointed out, "There are no personal problems, only potential marketing opportunities."

**A NEW KIND OF PARTY ANIMAL**

At the Democratic convention in Chicago, nothing really *happened.* In the media rooms outside the United Center, a radio talk-show host leaned over to a high school senior from inner-city Chicago, who was covering the goings-on for his school paper, and asked, "What have you learned, young man?" The kid looked at him balefully. "That this thing is useless," he answered.

There wasn't much for anyone under thirty-six to identify with. No new faces appeared at the podium, just worn Democratic visages like Jesse Jackson, Senator Barbara Boxer, and the president of the AFL-CIO. And then, there were the commercials.

The usual suspects made speeches. In this city of young neighborhoods, the Democratic Party continuously ran television ads about the threat of Medicare cuts. Wizened women hobbled across screens. Jerry Morrison, watching this on the TV at a Wicker Park coffeehouse, couldn't believe it. This didn't match up with the Democrats' strategy of getting out the youth vote like they had in 1992. "If this is the best reason they can give to vote," he said, stirring a mug of tea, "then the Dems really don't want young people to get out there in November." Suddenly, he realized that that was it. He leaned back in the wooden seat, momentarily stunned. It wasn't 1992 anymore. *"They don't want young people voting,"* he said slowly. "Too many of us are registering independent. We're a crapshoot. If they don't know exactly how you're going to go, they don't want you." The Democrats obviously felt they didn't need to cultivate the eighteen to thirty-five segment. After all, 1998, the year the youth vote would comprise the largest age voting bloc, seemed to be a very far two years away. Jerry shook his head and then straightened his union pin and prepared to go back to the United Center. After all, this was just one battle. The war was long.

The hallways were jammed with people in sequined hats and jackets made out of the stars and stripes, and "Gore 2000" placards swung in waves on the convention floor. This was especially interesting since at a rally for him earlier in the week, 300 young people had to be bribed with T-shirts by campaign volunteers and then bused in to chant and cheer. It looked good for television, but it was only screen deep.

"Can anyone find anything for real in this?" I asked. We had just sat through the vice president's speech that damned teen smoking—an irrefutably good stand, but basically meaningless.

"You're kidding, right?" Shawn Bullard laughed, not unkindly. After working four years for a conservative Democratic congressman, the thirty-one-year-old now did press relations for a lobbying firm in Washington. "The only way these guys are going to get real is if we get a few brewskies down 'em."

"I was thinking it might take something stronger," Lynn said.

Jonathan Hoyt, a twenty-six-year-old aide at the Department of Education, shook his head sadly. "All I know is, Gore better stop talking about cigarettes and better get religious about entitlements and crime if he wants to be around in four years." And then we all wandered off to the Philip Morris party. Philip Morris was known to throw blowouts, and the one at the Democratic convention lived up to all expectations. Even Gore's staffers could attest to that.

The Republican convention, held two weeks before in San Diego, had offered a "Youth Pavilion." The stage was outside the convention hall, surrounded on three sides by the Pacific Ocean. A huge screen stood at one side, flashing campaign quips and interviews. Red, white, and blue banners flapped in the wind. Beanbags littered the front of the stage, while bleachers were stacked on all sides. Nearly every hour, senators, congressmen, consultants, and candidates trooped to the stage for panel discussions on the economy, crime, environment, education, entitlements, and the media. Over four hundred people between sixteen and twenty-five had been recruited to attend. Even so, the phrase "the-Republican-Party-believes" rarely came into play. Instead, most speakers offered a variation of "here's-the-situation" and then patiently sat while audience members lined up behind three microphones to ask questions. Of course, the Youth Pavilion turned a bit surreal when Rachel from MTV's *Real World* San Francisco cast hosted a discussion with former presidential candidate Lamar Alexander on a purple velvet couch.

The GOP was just as adept as the Democrats at marketing. There was Elizabeth Dole's "let-me-tell-you-about-this-man-I-married" speech and Congresswoman Susan Molinari's keynote speech on being a mother and a Republican. The Republicans might have packaged *too* well, though. *Nightline* anchor Ted Koppel got so frustrated with the four-night extended commercial that he packed up his crew and left town early. NBC opted to broadcast a *Seinfeld* rerun instead of the acceptance speech of the vice presidential nominee, Jack Kemp. As a result, the combined three-network audience fell 25 percent from 1992.

And then, on the last day of the convention, Robert George stormed out of the center and smack into me. "Oh. Sorry," he muttered with only the most fleeting flicker of recognition. Forget the fact we had been playing phone tag since the convention kicked off. I would have brought this up, except Robert nearly had steam coming out of his ears.

"Are you okay?" I asked.

"No. No. I'm not okay. I'm pretty pissed off, actually." Each word shot out. He sucked in a deep breath. "Where are you headed?"

"The Youth Pavilion. They have free Diet Cokes there. But maybe you need something stronger."

Robert managed a small smile, walking in bounding steps next to me. "I've had it with politics," he said. I didn't believe him. This guy probably wore boxer shorts with little elephants on them. He wrote the Speaker's editorials. He had "no limit" virtually stamped on his forehead. But Robert grimaced.

*The Selling of the Press-ident*

"Two things just happened," he said. "Maybe if they hadn't happened one right after the other, I wouldn't have noticed so much." He shifted a stack of papers under one arm as we went through the security area. The guards grinned pleasantly. "First, I'm in this meeting for all the Speaker's staff, and the Speaker's political advisor was handing out little gifts to each of us. You know, little joke presents like plastic toy soldiers to thank us for all our hard work. I briefly had gotten up from my chair, and he accidentally skipped over me. I cleared my throat facetiously to point this out. He handed me a toy, saying, 'Oh, I didn't notice.' And as he turned away, he said, 'There goes our affirmative action.' This was in a room of about thirty people. I was one of only two black people there. It may have been a joke, but in the context of that room, it was incredibly inappropriate.

"Well, then, the Speaker was going to sign the welfare bill. You know, nice photo op to round off the convention. There was a group of us in the room, and Gingrich is sitting at a table, his pen out and the photographer ready to snap pictures. And then the Speaker says, 'Uh, Robert, why don't you come over by me and get in the picture?' I didn't move. I said, 'Thank you, but I'd rather not.' He said, 'Okay,' and turned to two women in the room and said, 'Why don't you get in the picture?' And they did. Afterward, one of the women came up to me and said, 'That took a lot of guts.' Well, I don't particularly enjoy being a prop. How convenient to have the black guy near you when you're signing the welfare bill."

His mouth tightened at the corners. "You know, to watch the convention is to think that twenty-five percent of the party is black. Every time the cameras pan to the audience, they go to a black face. Black people *are* Republicans. But why is it that the Republican Party feels it needs to go for the hard sell: 'Look how diverse we are!' We're so worried about focus groups, pundits, and polls that we're not really telling people what we're about."

Robert stopped, a few feet from the Youth Pavilion stage. There

*A NEW KIND OF PARTY ANIMAL*

was a break in the program, so only a few stagehands milled around. "The first night, we put a little girl up at the podium to tell the world she had AIDS. And how convenient she was also black. Yeah, that's sad. But what does that have to do with the election? Why aren't we talking about real things? Why are we doing all this touchy-feely stuff? We're cheating people when we do that. It's not about image. We need to be talking *real*."

He stared morosely out into the San Diego bay. The sun glittered on the surface.

"I came to Washington to deal with reality," he said. "If we're just supposed to wash it over with some nice photos and cute lines, I'll go somewhere else."

One of the Youth Pavilion coordinators trotted over to him. "Robert, hi!" he piped. "Can you come over and talk to some of these kids about what it's like working for the Speaker?"

Robert sighed, straightened his shoulders, and headed toward the little group clustered on beanbags.

Meanwhile, Alan Wheat of the Clinton-Gore campaign told the *Chicago Tribune*, "Young people can look at TV commercials and see through anything that [is] phony. They are looking for real accomplishment." Wheat's accomplishment was that he managed to say this without the slightest trace of irony.

———

Every time-honored tactic held dear by both parties—scandal-mongering, finger-pointing, decrying the decline in morality—and what happened when they flung these, full force, at 18–35s? Nothing. Only the deadened stare young people usually reserved for watching nature documentaries on mute while Pearl Jam blasted on a stereo in the background. "Well," said GOP consultant Mary Matalin at a Capitol Hill luncheon, shrugging, "maybe these guys are just up for grabs."

*The Selling of the Press-ident*

The thick hides of 18–35s truly baffled the political establishment. When, in 1996, a former Secret Service agent released a scathing book about his days in the Clinton White House, even young Republicans like Bob Meagher brushed it off. "Oh, a scandal in the White House," he scoffed. "Like *that's* never happened before."

It was the luck of the draw that 18–35s came of age during an era of political fallibility. And as a result, most had gone deaf on the subject of "character" a long time ago. Unlike older voters, they didn't necessarily *have* to feel tingly about a politician's morality. They had to feel confident about his abilities. This was something new and different for the political establishment that had operated on the supposition that voters needed to feel good about a candidate's person, no matter how intimate the detail. This was a trend born in the wake of Watergate. Wilbur Mills lost the chairmanship of the House Ways and Means Committee in 1974 when he was pulled over by police near the Jefferson Memorial, and a stripper happened to be in the car (she dove into the Tidal Basin in a futile attempt to escape). Congressman Wayne Hays had to resign from office in 1976 when his mistress revealed that she couldn't type but was still on his payroll. By the 1980s, sex was considered a viable issue in the character debate, and anyone who thought differently only needed to look at what had happened to Gary Hart. In the 1988 Democratic presidential primary, Hart challenged journalists to check the quality of his character—never a brilliant tactic. Within a few weeks, newspapers ran photos of the senator from Colorado snuggling with model Donna Rice on a boat called (of course) *Monkey Business*. With scenarios like this—Charles Dickens couldn't have wrapped it up so well—no wonder 18–35s grew up dismissing the "character issue." The rest of the public, though, was appalled. Gary Hart dropped out of the race. And from then on, the "character issue" was always brought up by commentators and consultants. It was the chorus to Bill Clinton's campaign in 1992, when his marital indiscretions, charges of smoking marijuana, draft dodging—not to mention protests against the Vietnam War—conspired to make him the character issue cover boy. It was Newt Gingrich's turn when he became the first Republican Speaker of the House in forty years. His divorce and his million-dollar book deal called his "character" into question.

A whole new take on "character" would emerge on the day of the president's acceptance speech at the Democratic convention. As Clinton rattled off a lengthy list of "little" promises like "targeted" tax cuts for education, child care, and jobs, his press secretary was busy explaining to reporters how the man who had helped craft that speech, the chief campaign strategist, Dick Morris, had resigned from his position after a supermarket tabloid published a story on his trysts with a $200-an-hour call girl. It seemed that the "character issue" no longer affected just the candidates, but their associates as well.

The character question gave Lee Atwater his career. The late GOP operative firmly believed in the beauty of opposition research. Digging up dusty records and uncovering "character issue" gems like mental illness, alcoholism, and adultery, Atwater helped candidates win race after race. Arguably, his finest moment came in 1988. He twisted the Massachusetts gubernatorial record of Democratic presidential candidate Michael Dukakis into the infamous Willie Horton commercial. The frames of a wild-eyed black man, a convicted murderer who still got weekend furloughs and raped a woman during one of them, were a smash with Atwater's peers. Forget the pesky fact that the furlough policy had been started by Dukakis's Republican predecessor.

The people Atwater hired to huddle in the basement of the Republican National Committee (opposition research wasn't the sole domain of the Republicans—the Democratic National Committee did it, too) were mostly 18–35s. Who else would work insane hours for virtual slave wages? Who else had an innate savvy of pitch? Of course 18-35s could successfully feed reporters juicy tidbits that garnered headlines. Throughout his two years at the Republican Senatorial Campaign Committee, a twenty-four-year-old opposition researcher from Mississippi wrapped his beige cubicle in yellow crime scene tape. He was only half joking. "The things we find out and leak to the press," he said, shaking his head. He didn't have to fabricate information. Few politicos had gone through their lives unblemished. But, the young man knew that the trick to selling this and getting actual coverage came down to a careful turn of phrase. "With most of these reporters, it's amazing. All we have to do is attach the suffix 'gate' and suddenly these guys are writing front-page stories that make our opponents look bad."

This tactic came almost effortlessly for an age group that was the first to grow up bombarded by slick advertisement campaigns on all sides: billboards, magazines, radio, television. The media primarily conveyed the message that you, too, could enjoy a happy life just by having these products. This might have worked on 18–35s during childhood, but they had figured it out by the time they were teens. When they hit their early twenties, and advertisers, who had grown up when television was new, pitched products with themes of alienation (Coca-Cola used the catchy phrase "What's the point of anything?" in 1994) and grating faux grunge (Burger King featured "BKTV" in 1991), "it may have been the most expensive marketing mistake in history," said an advertising executive. By 1997, the most successful campaigns would resemble the Nike magazine ad that read, "Don't insult our intelligence. Tell us what it is. Tell us what it does. And don't play the national anthem while you do it." That was not to imply that 18–35s were less patriotic than flag-factory-touring George Bush; they just didn't believe buying a certain product would make them patriotic.

The 18–35s also didn't have to be coached on sound bites, like older Americans did. They spoke in crisp, catchy sentences as a matter of natural course, even if they did slip in a few words of slang here and there. And, young people knew how media hype worked. They had come of age immersed in it. This was how hype worked: Reporters locked on to a person, built him up, and then systematically tore him down. Whether this was because of the abundance of different media venues within television, magazines, newspapers, radio, and the Internet or because the boomer-dominated journalists continued to be consumed by the question of "character" didn't really matter. The 18–35s saw this happen to enough people that they became skeptical whenever the media hailed the Next Great Thing. Oliver Stone, who wore his genera-tional status like a badge, grinned from glossy magazine covers one year, and was derided as a fanatical conspiracy theorist the next. Or, take the seemingly kindly curmudgeon Andy Rooney, the *60 Minutes* commentator styled to appear like everyone's uncle, with tweed coats and unruly eyebrows. "He's a *jerk*," muttered the inner-city high schooler who met Rooney while covering the Democratic convention. Most infamously, Rooney had vented his spleen on the magazine show about the suicide of Kurt Cobain. In Chicago, he brushed off any approach by teenaged journalists, snapping, "You call that a question?" Then, of course, from the 18–35s' own peer pool, there was Nancy Kerrigan and Eddie Vedder—lauded, then lambasted. It only further sharpened their dubiousness.

"*I'm* skeptical when I'm pitching something," said a twenty-four-year-old in public relations. "I can't afford to make pop gen-eralities," a consultant at BKG Youth once said, giving up after an exhaustive study. "I can't tell you a hundred ways to market to them. I can't boil it down to 'don't smile.'" And, in fact, the young opposition researchers didn't bother targeting their own peers. "Hell, yes, we're smarter than this stuff," said the twenty-four-year-old opposition researcher. "We don't actually *watch* these commercials." Then again, 18–35s don't watch television the way their parents do. Their parents follow scheduled programming. A Wednesday night show is seen on Wednesday night. But 18–35s are more inclined to tape a week's worth of television programs on their VCRs and watch when they have the time—*and* fast-forward through the commercial breaks. The younger half of this age bloc can barely recall the time when VCRs and television remote controls didn't exist.

James Carville thought he knew how to get them. In his book, *All's Fair*, cowritten with his wife, Mary Matalin, Carville detailed the shaping of "the message" in 1992, how painstakingly Clinton's staff picked out the tie he wore for the *Arsenio Hall Show:* "They . . . picked the loudest one for the governor to wear. . . . This may seem like frivolous image-crafting but in fact they were helping him in ways people don't see. It wasn't only that they wanted him to look more hip; they knew him well enough that this was going to symbolize their message to him: 'Don't listen to the old stiff guys who are telling you to act like you've got a corncob up your ass.'"

"We've been *had!*—how could we have been so stupid?" railed Kim Alexander, out in Sacramento where she was working on the first-ever voting guide on the Internet. She had no way of knowing that across the country, from Jerry Morrison in Chicago to Lynn Marquis in Washington to Charles McKinney in Durham, many of her peers thought the same thing. "We know better," she said. "We can tell when they're just saying what their consultants have told them to say. We have a responsibility to call them on this!" By 1994, 18–35s—Clinton's most solid voting-age block—had become his least stable. And by 1996, most young people had given up on both major parties.

So the "character issue" came up again. That was what the GOP crowed, anyway. But *character* wasn't the issue. *Issues* were the issue. In 1996, Global Strategy and Luntz Research both found that over 48 percent of eighteen- to thirty-five-year olds rank a candidate's position on specific issues to be the most important factor. If the parties didn't get this, MTV did—immediately. Before the 1996 campaign, the network hired two former Clinton White House staffers to beef up its coverage and rolled out its $800,000 Choose or Lose bus to traverse the country and pump up the youth vote. The interior looked like a three-dimensional fashion show: leopard-skin carpets, mosaic-tiled cabinets, gilt-framed windows, maroon wallpaper, a zebra-striped couch for interviews. The bus also had a full editing room under its silver star-spangled roof. Maybe the hipness of the Choose or Lose bus confused the other television networks, since a producer at *The NBC Nightly News* with Tom Brokaw remarked, "[MTV] shouldn't feel the pressure to do issue-oriented news."

"We don't look to the networks for advice," retorts MTV News producer Dave Anderson, who traveled with the bus through the country. "We've won a loyal audience by doing issue-oriented news." And in particular, news that 18–35s cared about. Anderson could have rattled off a synopsis to the networks. Coastal kids wanted to hear about the environment. Urban kids wanted to hear about crime. Midwest kids wanted to hear about education. And, they all wanted to hear about the job market and the economy.

The other networks did look to MTV, throwing their own young commentators on to the screen. Most of them were intelligent and well-qualified, but the wacky cross-cutting camera angles that accompanied them completely negated these qualities. The network powers must have been convinced they needed to imitate a music video instead of actually saying something informative. Worse still, when they let their youthful pundits speak, according to former CNN commentator Farai Chideya, "Our analysis was no different from anyone else's. When [anchors] Bernie Shaw and Judy Woodruff asked us questions, it was like, 'Here's our little pipsqueaks! They're so cute!' And we'd make a Pearl Jam reference, playing up to Gen-X-pectations . . . we should have had thongs and breast plates. It was just marketing, getting boomers to think the station is hip."

Even with all the polls showing that 18–35s wanted substance, no one—not the candidates, not the media—really addressed specifics like Ross Perot did in 1992. Perot didn't aim his infomercial strategy specifically at them. He was going for the disenfranchised voter in general. Other politicians could have followed this model in 1996. They did declare that they would "run on the issues," eschewing the usual mudslinging. But to the political establishment, "running on the issues" meant sketching a topic instead of painting it in depth. At the town hall meeting presidential debate, Clinton and Dole were asked about the looming problem of Social Security. Dole answered by telling the audience how much his mother liked receiving her monthly check. Clinton answered with smooth, empty words that assured—in a roundabout way—he wouldn't change a thing but understood their concern. One of the most enlightening moments of the debate came at the end, when Dole announced that his closing words were directed to the youth of America. Could it be that the World War II veteran was finally going to prove he had some idea of what they cared about? Well, not exactly. "Just don't do it," he babbled, a weak takeoff of Nancy Reagan's antidrug mantra from the 1980s. Nothing offered by the establishment was real anymore. After years of spinning and media coaching, politicians knew only how to utter words of plastic.

———

As she did nearly every morning, Kim Alexander stepped over vagrants to get to the doorway of her office building. They slumped in matted, greasy lumps, just four blocks from the state capitol, surrounded by pawnshops and bail-bond kings. Sacramento was still a Gold Rush town—not because of the wooden sidewalks and false fronts of the "Old Sac" section, jammed with junky little tourist stores. It was the capital of the largest state, in terms of population and electoral votes, in the most powerful country in the twentieth-century world, at the very forefront of the cyber revolution.

And Kim had an organizational weapon that no previous generation had ever possessed. The Internet was high tech word-of-mouth. At the California Voter Foundation, where Kim was executive director, she dealt with the public marketplace, where the contest was clear-cut: Provide information that is accurate, accessible, and first and you win; let the competition define it first and you lose. Accessibility depended a lot on the quality of a user's modem, since crashes happened frequently and graphics could be irritatingly slow to upload. But once one was on the Internet, a site had to be dependably and uniquely informative in order to rally a loyal audience. Kim thought she could pull this off. Once she did, she knew—and this was an absolute—that she had the key to use the Internet to transform politics.

Her peers wanted to be involved. They wanted to be active. They just didn't have an outlet they trusted. Anything said by politicians or the mainstream media was never taken at face value. Kim *knew* this as sure as there were fish in the ocean. But then, she'd known this two years ago when she worked at the nationally known watchdog group Common Cause. She told anyone who would listen that she thought the 18–35 vote should be cultivated.

"You're crazy," scoffed one politico. "They just want to sit on the couch, watch commercials, and wait for the mail to come, just like everybody else."

"You're way too idealistic," said another. "That's just so far-fetched."

Kim rolled her eyes and walked away from the naysayers. She wasn't easily convinced. She had heard this type of talk before. When she attended the University of California at Santa Barbara and worked with other students to bring about divestment of the UC system in South Africa, adults derided their attempts as "unrealistic." Of course, that was exactly what the UC system ended up doing, but who was keeping score? Kim considered herself "realistic with high expectations." There was nothing wrong with that. And *why* was it so crazy to think voters—young voters—could be proactive? Kim demanded an answer from her friends, who she figured would offer up the truth. Was her gut feeling right or not? As it ended up, they didn't think she was off base, but then again they were Net-heads, like her. Unlike the zipkids in the Silicon Valley, who pulled and played with the technology, Kim's crowd was about content. So, they listened to her idea about the Internet.

"People vote based on where they live," she said. "People our age are so transitory, moving around from job to job, coming and going all the time. Previous generations lived in one place most of their lives, so politicians had time to cultivate them. That isn't reality now. So what if, when you moved into a new area, you could go on-line and find out who your representatives are, their voting records, addresses, what special interest groups endorse and oppose them, *just by typing in your new zip code?*" Kim waited a moment. "I think we'd vote. I think we'd participate and even use this to exchange ideas with young people in other states."

"I think you are just a continual stream," Ron Gray said, shaking his head. The thirty-five-year-old political consultant figured he heard about five ideas a day out of her. "How does your brain not explode?"

But Kim was launched on this one, which, as Ron knew, could be lethal. You didn't work in the boiling hot seat of the California senate and then at Common Cause without learning that you couldn't shoot your mouth off. Kim had come out of those jobs with steeled nerves and hardened will. Oh, she still looked soft enough—her face round and smooth under auburn hair cropped at the chin. She was thirty and would have seemed even younger if

A NEW KIND OF PARTY ANIMAL

not for the fierce intensity that drew up her small frame and lit her cerulean eyes with fire.

Her initial attempt at an on-line guide would be one of the first political sites ever. "File that one away for Trivial Pursuit," she told her friends. For the 1994 midterm election, she gathered candidates' biographies, platform papers, endorsement lists, speeches and press releases. It didn't do too badly for a first-time effort. It was accessed 14,000 times and registered over 36,000 file retrievals. And, of course, Kim learned. Since press releases were the least likely to be pulled up, those would not be included in future guides. The news articles from the California *Journal,* a nonpartisan monthly public policy magazine, proved extremely popular. She would get the *Journal*'s ballot measure analysis in each subsequent on-line guide, and a race-by-race breakdown by 1996.

Her second go-round was the San Francisco Online Voter Guide for the 1995 mayoral election. This one featured the first Internet database of campaign contributions and expenditures. The San Francisco guide registered over 23,000 file retrievals. *PC Magazine* rated it as one of the top 100 Web sites of 1995. So, Kim had high expectations for the 1996 guide.

Oh, sure, Internet voting guides still had a long way to go. But for now, one thing was certain: Kim had proven that cyberspace was a viable source of information that was not the drivel turned out by campaign directors, consultants, pundits, and reporters; it was a sanctuary away from the hype. The nonissue of "character" could be filtered out in favor of more tangible items, like interactive on-line audiences with candidates (as opposed to passively listening to a television anchor asking prefabricated questions), lengthy explanations on positions (instead of making do with sound bites), and posted career voting records to scroll through (without waiting for a press secretary to release a selected few to the public). No wonder most of the people tapping into it were young. *Viva la revolucion,* she thought, and gleefully turned on her computer.

That same month, Sam Donaldson faced a room of eager-eyed interns. They had spent the summer working for free on Capitol Hill, doing unpleasant tasks like dealing with angry constituent phone calls and filing endless reams of paper. Their reward had been a series of lectures. Cabinet secretaries spoke. James Carville addressed them. And now, Sam Donaldson. The Cannon Caucus Room, glittering in its crystal finery, was crowded with twenty-year-olds who were just days away from packing off to their final two years of college. The young men wore the unofficial intern uniform of khaki slacks and blue blazers. The young women wore whatever had been offered that season by The Limited.

"I'll answer any questions," Sam Donaldson said. "You want to know about journalism? I'll tell you. You want to know what Diane Sawyer's really like? I'll tell you."

One of them wanted to know what he thought of the Internet as a news source. Hardly a surprise, since 98 percent of four-year colleges give students Internet access, and 60 percent of 18–35s own a personal computer, the highest of any age group. All at once, Sam Donaldson stopped smiling. His face flushed dark red, then purple, then red again. The sixty-two-year-old who had spent more years in the news business in Washington than the oldest of this generation bellowed, "You want to know what I think? I see things on the Internet that I couldn't say—calling politicians names, slanderous names. They should be subjected to libel laws. Hold them responsible!"

Sam Donaldson shook his head dismissively. "I don't attach any value to the Internet," he said.

Then again, when Sam Donaldson came of age, Walter Cronkite would pour himself a cup of coffee each weekday morning, spread *The New York Times* across his desk, and begin to line up stories for the CBS Evening News. Of course, the events of the day could alter this—catastrophes like a crash or a shooting—but basically, national news was what Cronkite chose to pass along to everyone else from his hometown newspaper. And, newspapers and network television had the power to set an agenda. Any industry list of the "most influential" papers would begin with the big three—the *Times, The Wall Street Journal, The Washington Post*—and then move to the big regionals—*The Boston Globe, The Miami Herald,* the *Chicago Tribune,* and so on. Television consisted of ABC, CBS, and NBC.

When the 18–35s came of age, cable television arrived, and Rupert Murdoch created Fox, a full-fledged, non-cable network to compete with the big three. These young people couldn't identify with fond references to "Uncle Walter." Cronkite had vacated his anchor seat in 1981. And the major newspapers no longer had a lock, either. *USA Today,* which defined not a geographical market but a demographical one, clutched a large enough audience to rank fourth in the nation.

As network ratings fell from 43.2 percent in 1994 to 40.6 in 1995, and cable rose from 14.1 to 17.1, the media decried the information dearth among young people: Allegedly, they didn't watch the news. When the Pew Research Center in Washington found that 22 percent of Americans under thirty said they regularly watched a network news broadcast in 1996, down from 36 percent in 1995, the study's director concluded that "young people today are less interested in serious news than previous generations of young people." But then, this assumes that the network news is the "serious" news. Several polls done the same year found that 85 percent of 18–35s watched their *local* television news three times a week, and over 70 percent cited *local* news as their source of choice. Then again, most 18–35s weren't home in time to catch the 6:30 P.M. network broadcasts. Local news aired between 10 and 11 P.M. And as for the accusation that young people didn't read (the *Los Angeles Times* ran an editorial in 1992—"Yo, Kids"—

that condescended by saying, "Unfortunately, many watch little besides popular TV shows or read anything longer than a CD lyric sheet"), marketing studies found that they spent more of their disposable income on information sources than any other age group.

What the media powers-that-be have not fully realized is that for the information-driven (and -drenched) society of 18–35s, packaging is not as important as content. A nightly news broadcast filled with quips and zippy camera angles will be sidestepped for quality news that is available around the clock, both on television and through the Internet. This is a result of being the first generation to grow up with computers—much as their parents were the first to grow up with television. The "fear of technology," which so strikes older age groups, has not been a factor for young Americans, although getting carpel tunnel syndrome before acne has been. Parents of 18–35s initially restricted their understanding of their children's use of computers to video games. Pac Man fever had gripped them. A story on Space Invaders done by a Los Angeles television news reporter in 1983 ended with the reporter saying seriously, "Experts say that if future wars are waged in space, this generation will be ready." Adults also decided that if young people weren't playing video games, they were hacking into confidential files and generally creating a nuisance, images promoted by techno-kids-run-amok movies like *WarGames* in the 1980s and *Hackers* in the 1990s.

Meanwhile, in the real world, 18–35s designed software, fiddled with chips, and began to map a giant unknown called "the Web." By the 1990s, they didn't simply use the World Wide Web—they were *building* it. Across the country, young people started Internet companies, published Web 'zines, and produced sites. And before most Americans even remotely understood what was going on, 18–35s had redefined "effective" news. This used to mean delivering a targeted message to a carefully selected audience. But 18–35s—and the generation coming up behind them—

can decide whether or not they *want* to access the message. This is the way the Internet empowers. People are no longer dependent on those who usually control the information flow. Anyone can access whatever information they want, from almost any place they want, without a Walter Cronkite deeming whether or not it is important. "By spring '96," observed digital writer Jon Katz, "I couldn't bear the *New York Times* pundits, CNN's politico-sports talk, the whoring Washington talk shows, the network stand-ups. Why attend to those tired institutions when what was happening on the monitor a foot from my nose seemed so much more interesting?" Maybe this is why most people tend to believe what they read on the Internet, even if there is no source cited. When less than half of Americans of all ages believe what the media tells them, it shouldn't be too surprising that, for 18–35s, the Internet had become the way to get raw, honest, and fast information.

Abbie Hoffman's peers talked about revolution. Netscape founder Marc Andreessen's are making it. The unhindered access to almost all of the world's information has given way to the ever-evolving, independent political identity of 18–35s. Historian Hannah Arendt once wrote that the sudden experience of being free and the sense of creating something are the two things necessary to bring about revolutions. The Internet hits both of those.

Two months after Sam Donaldson's meeting with the Capitol Hill interns, I ran in to him at the Democratic National Convention. He sat in a plush chair in the ABC Skybox, relaxing before the crush of politicians and delegates inevitably wandered through. I reminded him of the Internet question: What did he think of it as a news source? This time, his face didn't turn into a color swatch. Instead, he smiled sweetly.

"I say," he answered, "let all flowers bloom."

———

To understand marketing is to see how Quillie and Charles broke down the politics of crime.

The real issue: homicide by youths under seventeen tripled between 1984 and 1994; juvenile arrest rates for weapons-law violations increased 103 percent between 1985 and 1994; juvenile offenders were responsible for 14 percent of all violent crime and one-fourth of all property crime. ("At some point," Charles admitted, "you do say, 'That guy doesn't need a program; he needs *parole.*'")

The way it was sold: President Clinton vowed to punish "thirteen-year-olds . . . with automatic weapons." *Rolling Stone* magazine declared, "The disease is adolescence." The headline of *U.S. News and World Report* magazine screamed: "Teen Crime Bomb."

What Quillie and Charles knew: Clinton's peers, fifty-year-old men, murdered twice as many people each year as thirteen-year-olds with automatic weapons. And if "the disease is adolescence" ("It's not exactly like we can *fix* that or there's a way around it," Charles snapped), then why was the drug death rate among the peers of *Rolling Stone* publisher Jann Wenner fifteen times that of adolescents? And Wenner could hardly say that the eighty-month average for marriage among his peers, or the record number of child abandonments and deadbeat dads, or the full half who admitted to illegal drug use, extramarital sex, and drunk driving was *healthy.* Somehow, so-called grown-ups overlooked the fact that they themselves committed 87 percent of violent crimes—and that included six out of ten crimes committed against children.

Conclusion: Screw the kids, then blame the kids, and for God's sake, package it well.

Children were a malleable marketing tool, though. Scapegoat them when you needed one bill passed, deify them when you needed to get another bill through. There is no better example of the art of spin than how politicians of every persuasion have used "but-I'm-doing-this-to-protect-children" as their catchall pitch to make their agenda into law. Clinton didn't pass his universal health coverage in 1993, so he retooled it as universal coverage for children in 1997. Antiabortionists got around the accusation that they invaded the private lives of women by saying they were protecting "preborn children." Republicans who wanted to cut school lunches and food stamps (which benefit children) said they were only doing so to balance the budget for the sake of future children. A washing machine has a gentler spin cycle.

The concept of "spin," which is really just another way of saying "ignore the facts—here's the real truth," shot up to new extremes during the hearings held by the Senate Governmental Affairs Committee in July 1997. For nearly two months, the hearings ostensibly explored the finance abuses of the 1996 campaign season. But even as committee chairman Fred Thompson (a former movie actor, no less) questioned witnesses in his sonorous baritone, a clutch of Democratic spin doctors were stationed outside the hearing room doors, offering instant, glossy assessments as each word of testimony was uttered. "I'm having fun," the president's scandal control specialist exulted to reporters. Of course, many journalists did observe in their articles the absurdity of this spin excess. But, that overlooks a crucial point: The media still flocked to the spinners, and it quoted whatever they said. No wonder so many young people consider news as it comes down through television, magazines, and newspapers to be prepackaged drivel. Reporters might complain about being managed by press secretaries and scandal control specialists, but they don't stop going to them for quotes. Imagine, then, what the campaign finance hearings might have been like if journalists had spotted the cadre of spin doctors in the hall and *had walked past them without stopping*. With that one sweeping gesture, reporters would have clearly signaled that the days of politicos shepherding them along with careful words and phrases were over. Instead, of course, it was business as usual, and the spinmeisters kept up a roaring trade in the hallways of the Senate.

If young people in general are frustrated about this, imagine the reaction of eighteen- to thirty-five-year-old press secretaries, who have firsthand knowledge of the art. It used to be that this position was reserved for hardened, crusty, media veterans who knew the power brokers, had carbon-stained fingers in their early careers, and still drank their whiskey straight up. These men (and they were almost always men) did not come cheap. Their average salary was $50,000 a year. As congressional offices dealt with shrinking budgets, many representatives discovered that they could hire newly minted college graduates as press secretaries. Not only did the members end up with inherently media savvy staffers, but the latter were a lot less expensive than their older counterparts. In 1993, when the trend toward young press secretaries began, the average starting salary was $22,000. After all, as *USA Today* had proclaimed, it was "The Worst Job Market for College Grads Ever."

I was one of the first twenty-two-year-olds in the job. "You're going to get eaten alive," warned a forty-year-old communications director who feared for me among a Washington press corps renowned for its scorpion pens. I survived. And even though I worked for a wonderful congressman who believed in the truth above all, it was more than a little disconcerting to watch as an enormous wash of pie charts, statistics, polls, studies, various budget outlines, and proposed amendments flowed through the office, knowing that this would never make it unfiltered into the outside world. My young colleagues also became more disenchanted with each passing week as they managed the news from their bosses' offices. "It is so depressing," one told me, "to realize that we hold so much back. Classified stuff, I can understand. But I'm having to keep other things from people, like tax information and defense deals. It makes me wonder: If I'm not telling everything, what are others not telling me?"

The cherry on this sundae was legions of so-called experts who descended on a topic like the crusaders galloping toward Galilee. As if the layers and layers of people deciding "what was news" wasn't bad enough, there were still more who told the public what to think *about* the news. Kim, for one, considered the flimflam "generational spokespeople" to be the worst. She tried hard not to begrudge them—making a buck off your age wasn't a crime—but when some of them could only manage the most inane comments, she wanted to scream or laugh or tear out her hair. Every network seemed to have their own, but it got worse when MSNBC was launched in 1996. The president of NBC News, Andrew Lack, wanted to attract young viewers. He decided the new twenty-four-hour cable network should "re-create the relaxed feeling of a bull session with journalist friends." He came up with—yes, *The Friends*—a psuedo-cast of fledgling talking heads. MSNBC even had auditions for the "roles."

But instead of a well-informed news cast, MSNBC wound up with a well-informed opinion group dancing through an endless discussion on any subject. Lack never stopped to consider that 18–35s already got this when they went to coffeehouses *themselves* and were able to chat about issues *themselves*. Where was the fun or, more important, the productivity, in passively listening to other people (who were tagged as "former speechwriter" or "former counsel"—always a "former")? Most of MSNBC's commentators had the unfortunate trait of attempting to be experts on every-thing. One morning featured three youthful pundits discussing a judge who had ruled that parents who smoked around their asthmatic children were committing a form of abuse. None of the talking heads was married or had children or was even a lawyer (which at least would have allowed them to dissect the merits of the case). Instead, they argued for the sake of arguing in front of a camera. ("There's something incredibly titillating about the money and the adulation of television," one MSNBC pundit told a reporter, "but it has nothing to do with rising to the moral issue of your day.")

MSNBC is not alone in this practice. When pollster and consultant Kimberly Schuld was asked by Fox Morning News in Washington to "talk about Zaire," she replied, "Why? Why are you calling me? I don't know foreign policy." There is an expectation by producers that commentators, particularly young ones, must have something to say about everything. But, this is tiresome to watch. The viewing numbers back this up. By mid-1997, the Food Channel had a larger audience than MSNBC.

This is why the Internet is so important. "People have a voice again," Kim Alexander maintained. "They've forgotten how to use it, but they're figuring it out pretty fast."

While the media focused on the charge/countercharge debates between parties, slapping the suffix "gate" on to the slightest wrongdoing, and while consultants and marketing strategists tried to figure out new ways to sell their candidates, young people like Charles and Quillie, who wanted to know the reality behind the crime issue, quietly logged on to the World Wide Web.

Let the Carvilles and the Atwaters of politics think they are brilliantly pulling another one over on the public. Let the Rooneys and the Donaldsons expound on their interpretations of events. They clearly didn't get it, and, as Kim had warned, 18–35s could work around them. It was happening already.

## Chapter Five

# *CYBERPOL VALUES*

When Kim was in her twenties, she got religion. Most people her age did. She clicked on her Macintosh, and there it was, the Internet, glowing beatifically as it electrified her brain with fervor and inspiration. Of course there was no Church of the Internet— cyberspace didn't need a brick and mortar structure. A computer and modem were the necessary physical elements, and that was sufficient means to the end that Kim had in mind.

Nothing—not the bums lolling about and urinating in front of her office, not the constant lack of street parking in downtown Sacramento, not even unreliable modems (there were glitches along every holy road)—could roil Kim's blood like partisan politics. The rest she could usually handle. But the games the parties played had reached a point of no return. Kim, like most of her peers, would rather have leeches stuck all over her body than attempt a thankless task like unraveling the bitter finger-pointing, but too many other heads were popping up on the partisan Hydra.

Kim had come up with an idea that was going to get around the spineless public servants in the California state assembly and senate. You want change in politics? Then get 'em where it counts. Fund-raising. Nothing could foster change like publicly asking the question of money, and there was no better way than the Internet to keep track of monetary contributions to campaigns. In fact, if anything was going to usher in the Internet era of politics, it was going to be the age-old question: Who's buying influence with whom?

Kim knew 1996 would not be *the* campaign waged on the Internet. It was going to be more of a trial run. But, it would also be the last campaign in which the Internet was not a major factor. Kim leaned back in her chair again and smiled. Guess what age group was at the helm of the new technology and new media? Matthew Nelson was twenty-six when he started *Wired* magazine's Web site, HotWired. At thirty-one, Halsey Minor founded c/net, a computer version of CNN. And Marc Andreessen was only twenty-four when his company, Netscape Communications, had the most successful public offering in history—on the same day that Jerry Garcia died, the year-old company with no earnings was instantly valued at over $2 billion. It became a joke around Silicon Valley: What were Jerry Garcia's last words before his heart attack? "Netscape opened at *what?*" Andreessen's coworkers, John Mittelhauser, Chris Wilson, and Aleksandar Totic, were also in their twenties. *Newsweek* and other publications might label

Netscape "a two-year-old start-up company populated by wise-ass Gen-X millionaires who wear shorts to work," but the Net culture itself dismissed this. The people judging them didn't know *how* to judge them. While the kids coming up behind them—who were even more astute about technology—had to contend with nervous, Net-intimidated parents (who saddled their offspring with blocking software like Net Nanny and Cybersitter), the 18–35s paved the way.

They took cyberspace beyond a mere method to millions, though. This was the beginning stage of an emerging way of life. No wonder the Christian Coalition and other alleged "values" groups led the fight to censor the Internet. Never mind the fact that the national organization and many of the local chapters all had Web sites. The coalition had a values agenda to press. Among other measures, it supported prayer in school ("But what kind of prayer are you going to use?" Kim wondered. "Are you going to make a Baptist kid say a Muslim prayer?"), a ban on flag burning and abortion, and V chips for all televisions. By virtue of its name, the organization claimed to speak for all good, God-fearing Christian folk. The chutzpah of this aside, it did have nearly two million dues-paying members and chapters in all fifty states, mostly because of the indefatigable grassroots efforts of its thirty-five-year-old baby-faced executive director. Ralph Reed was a peer of Kim's in the sense of hands-on, local-based politics—the coalition's strength was derived largely from its ability to turn out voters on the local level, another staple of Reed's strategy. But when it came to the area of "values," Reed couldn't have been more different. The word had layers of meaning for his followers, from church to respect for elders to moral vision and obligation. Reed's own age group, though, was the least likely to identify themselves as "Christian conservatives." Only 6.3 percent thought that "family values" was the most important issue today. In a 1996 survey, 10.3 percent listed God as their hero, which tied the deity with

Hillary Rodham Clinton. And while 90 percent of 18–35s believed in a higher power, less than half ever or rarely attended church. They were building another structure.

Like Reed, Kim was doing it through politics. She thought the California Voter Foundation provided the perfect opportunity for trying to change politics through the Internet. The organization had been founded in 1989 by former California Secretary of State March Fong Eu, who wanted to increase voter registration. When Fong couldn't fund the program with private sources, and getting a tax exemption proved difficult, her office decided in 1994 to separate itself from the foundation. When Kim took over, she turned it into "a non-profit, non-partisan organization dedicated to informing the electorate through the Internet." At least, that was what the brochure said. As the executive director, she could apply her vision to what seemed at first glance to be a limited organization. Merely increasing voter registration wouldn't get more people involved in politics. After all, "involvement" meant more than a vote. It included education and participation through town hall meetings, letters, and monitoring legislation. Kim could accomplish this through the myriad possibilities that the Internet offered. If Ralph Reed could push evangelist Pat Robertson's mouthpiece into becoming a formidable organization consumed by domestic politics, Kim could achieve her comparatively humble goal.

"We are living in the information age; information is power; through information we will empower people" was her mantra. To the politicos who dismissed her as "hopeful" (and there were many), she snapped back, "If you're not hopeful, nothing's going to happen." Oh, yes, something was going to happen. Now that "devolution" had become hip, with the federal government handing over more and more power to state governments, it was especially important to keep tabs on what was going on. How many people out there knew who their state representatives were? Most barely

*A NEW KIND OF PARTY ANIMAL*

knew the names of their U.S. congressional representatives. The state officials seemed to like it this way. Every time legislation came up that might further educate the public, they killed it. Kim had watched as Sacramento knocked away not one or two but *four* attempts to pass electronic filing, which would have required candidates to list campaign contributions on the Internet. First the Democrats put up a bill and the Republicans buried it. Then the Republicans brought up their version and the Democrats destroyed it. And then an independent introduced his version and everyone defeated it.

The bastards thought they'd gotten away with it. Kim could see why they wouldn't want their campaign contributions on the Internet. The bill wouldn't have changed the official filing dates, but it would have opened up access. Right now, if a reporter or a citizen wanted to see who was buying influence with which representative, he would have to travel to the secretary of state's office in Sacramento and sift through several cubic feet of files. Not only was this time-consuming, it also wasn't feasible for most people. Electronic filing would require candidates to list their funds on the Internet, where anyone could tap on and read them. Kim called it "digital sunlight."

*Money* slipped and twisted through every political crevice. During the 1996 election, between both presidential campaigns, the Democrats and the Republicans brought in more than $262 million in "soft money," a conveniently cuddly term (like "friendly fire") to describe something less than palatable. Soft money, the unregulated, usually six-figure contributions from wealthy individuals, corporations, and labor unions, is supposedly given to the parties but *somehow* ends up in federal campaigns. The $262 million collected in 1996 was three times the amount of soft money raised four years earlier. Columnist George Will would brush off any concerns about this, saying that the amount of soft money spent in the 1992 congressional races equaled "40 percent of what

Americans spent on yogurt." Will's disregard aside, Clinton's re-election campaign proved to be a textbook case of the system's flaws. Political science professors would be teaching this one for years to come: a White House so consumed with raising the daunting multimillion amount necessary to run a presidential campaign, with $200,000 for coffee klatches and $100,000 for nights in the Lincoln bedroom and $300,000 for rides on Air Force One. All were legal but smacked vaguely of being unethical. And the vice president himself made a majority of fund-raising calls, which *was* illegal if he made them from a government build-ing. "Getting a call from Al Gore and getting a call from me are two different things," explained a Republican financier. "If I ask a guy for $100,000, the donor can tell me to go jump in a lake. When Al Gore does it, the donor can't say that, and he has to wonder, 'Does he have my privates in his hand?'"

But the most telling moment would be related by *New York Times* columnist William Safire, who wrote a piece about the pos-sibility of illegal foreign contributions given to the Clinton cam-paign. " . . . Silence from the Republicans," Safire wrote. "Not only were they not the original source of the story, they offered little newsworthy reaction. I ran into Haley Barbour, then chairman of the Republican National Committee . . . and put it to him: Did he have a statement? His reply: 'This is something for Ross Perot to hit hard.' That struck me as curious; why Perot, the third-party candidate—why not Dole and Barbour?" As Safire and the rest of the country later discovered, this was because Barbour had made his own foreign connection for the think tank that he headed. It was, Safire proclaimed, a "shell game."

The national press would spend a bit of 1996 and most of 1997 untangling contributions they labeled "questionable." But if every-thing had been listed on the Internet, the "scandal" never would have snowballed. The information would have been available to the wired public from the start, and that proximity might have

A NEW KIND OF PARTY ANIMAL

prompted politicians to be more scrupulous—or at least more cautious. Kim had a plan that would keep the California press from having to backtrack.

She *knew* it would work, just as surely as there were earthquakes in California. All the signs were there that politicians would have to be different, and soon. When she worked as a staff consultant in the state senate and watched as Bill Clinton continually chose between what he believed in and what was politically expedient (he always went with expediency, of course), her heart sank.

"Come on, Kim," a state lobbyist had said, "what did you expect? They all do this."

"It has to change," Kim had insisted. "This isn't good enough. We have to force the issue."

The price of taking the easy way out (which often was synonymous with taking dirty money) pushed the grains of faith even faster through the hourglass. Kim spent her free time registering her peers to vote. The last two rounds proved to be illuminating experiences, as she would dryly say. In 1992, they nearly jumped: "Show me where to sign!" But when 1996 rolled around, young people didn't sign up as Democrats or even as Republicans. Instead, they asked her, "Can I be my own party?" Kim herself was a Democrat, despite coming from a long line of Lincoln Republicans. But she had reregistered with the Reform Party in 1996. She didn't trust Clinton to stick to a course—any course, let alone the right one. Look what he'd done to Joycelyn Elders. When the Christian Coalition and other conservative groups criticized the former surgeon general for publicly supporting masturbation as an alternative to sexual intercourse (as if the Christian Coalition had any better, remotely realistic ideas!), Clinton almost immediately asked for her resignation. So maybe Joycelyn Elders didn't exactly say what was politically correct, but—oh, hell. At least she was trying to come up with solutions. Kim kicked back in her chair, still ticked off nearly two years later. She thought Elders had been one of the few inspiring people in the Clinton cabinet. She said what she believed. She wasn't afraid to be bold or controversial if that was what it took to find possible solutions to tricky problems —exactly the qualities that 18–35s looked for in a leader. And Clinton had thrown her out like a used rag. Clinton wasn't a different kind of politician at all.

Of course, this was before any questions of money came up. That would consume most of 1997. But in 1996, Kim tapped on her keyboard, thinking, *So,* the California legislature doesn't want to list their campaign contributions on the Internet? Well, the information was sitting in the secretary of state's office. What was stopping Kim—and the California Voter Foundation—from taking action into their own hands? She knew from working at Common Cause that the money that came in during the last two weeks of a campaign often decided the race. Candidates used it for that last-minute media blitz to get their names and their messages out. This strategy usually worked. As a result, late contributions had to be reported within twenty-four hours, but since that information was then dumped into overflowing three-ring binders, reporters rarely had the time to index all the names, addresses, occupations, and clients of all the contributors on the lists. In previous election cycles, if journalists ever got the information, they got it well after election day. So, Kim was going to help them out. She hired a cadre of interns, and every one of the final fourteen days they were going to go down to the secretary of state's office with laptops and flip through every contribution and send that information out on the Internet. If the legislature wouldn't do electronic filing itself, Kim was going to do it for them.

She had learned about campaign contributions early on. Her father had run for city council twice in Culver City. It only took a couple of thousand to run a campaign, and the second time around, a man offered Richard Alexander a $500 contribution.

**A NEW KIND OF PARTY ANIMAL**

Richard sent him away. "Kimmy," he said when she asked why, "if I took that man's money, I'd owe him something." He won, anyway, and served on the city council for sixteen years. Kim didn't object so much to the practice of giving money to campaigns or to support ballot measures. She didn't like the insidious secrecy surrounding it.

The state legislators liked it this way. When the concept of using the Internet was brought up, filing reports electronically and maintaining a centralized database that could make the information available to however many thousands or millions of people around California wanted it, the legislators killed four bills—wham, wham, wham, wham—that would have made it law.

"They're afraid," Ron Gray told Kim. He was a consultant and one of Kim's longtime friends. She had invited him and a few others over for dinner and to watch the local ten o'clock news.

Kim stirred a pot of tomato sauce while Ron leaned against the counter.

"They're all a bunch of jerks," she corrected. "PACs, soft money—it's like an air bubble under a carpet. You step on it in one place and it pops up somewhere else. There've always been sinister people trying to buy influence—"

"Sinister?" Ron asked. He had run enough campaigns to know how to argue this one. "How is it sinister to try and make a buck? These donors are trying to get a competitive edge. That's what capitalism is all about."

"Yeah, but, Ron, the legislators are constantly trying to figure out what they can get away with," Kim insisted. She had come to Sacramento on the heels of one of the biggest FBI sting operations ever. The FBI had been tipped off that business entities in California had to pay "entry fees" to state legislators, through campaign contributions or honoraria or other means. The bureau set up a dummy corporation—Peach State Capital—and posed as businessmen from Alabama who wanted tax exemptions to set up a shrimp-processing plant in Sacramento. From 1984 to 1986, they gave out tens of thousands of dollars in contributions in exchange for a special interest bill—that not only passed both houses of the legislature but also made it all the way to the governor's desk. The FBI had to tip *him* off to prevent him from signing it. The next day, the FBI staged a predawn raid on the state capitol. By the time staffers arrived, the place was wrapped in yellow crime scene tape. Fourteen legislators, aides, and lobbyists were arrested and convicted.

The FBI agents said they were stunned at how easy the whole thing had been. At any time, anyone—a reporter, for instance—could have looked at the legislators' campaign disclosures, seen the out-of-state contributions from Peach State Capital, and maybe wondered why a company from Alabama was supporting State Senator Joe Montoya from Los Angeles. The information was there, but it was buried in an avalanche of paper.

"If legislators had to report their contributions on the Internet within twenty-four hours, without a bazillion forms holding them up, that would be the best thing we could do to help them," Kim said. "The new democracy."

She didn't think Ron would buy this. He always tried to play the cynic to her idealist. But Ron smiled, his eyes crinkling at the corners. "Wouldn't it be cool," he said, "if *we* were the new democracy?"

———

"Jim is a wonderful guy."

That was the entire content of the Jim Cunneen Web site in 1996. The assemblyman from central California still wasn't convinced about the Internet as a political tool. Cunneen didn't have to worry. He was running unopposed. But on a national level, politicians took the Internet seriously. Some of them had young

*A NEW KIND OF PARTY ANIMAL*

aides pushing them into it. Others swung with the times themselves. Senator Patrick Moynihan, age sixty-nine, could be seen tapping on a laptop while flying between Washington and New York. And it was sixty-four-year-old Ted Kennedy who established the first congressional Web site early in his reelection campaign in 1994.

Informed political choice has always depended directly on what happens to be the capacity of the country's communications system. In the eighteenth century, politicians ran races for a small group of (according to the voting requirements of the time) white male property owners who usually knew them. Through the nineteenth and mid-twentieth centuries, this expanded beyond local contacts and face-to-face experiences to newspapers and radio, and then, after the 1950s, to television. Coming into the twenty-first century, the Internet rewrites all the rules. With it, distance no longer acts as an obstacle to forming political alliances. Electronic messages sent across the street or across the world are transmitted via satellite and arrive simultaneously, with equal timeliness. People can interact with others thousands of miles away as easily—or even *more* easily—as they interact with their next-door neighbors. While the Internet could provide a new way for politicians and constituents to actually engage in two-way conversations (possibly alleviating a little of the political alienation felt by most Americans), most politicos didn't get that far. After all, it was just in 1992 that "new media" had referred to cable channels and fax and 800 numbers. Erring on the side of caution, politicians stuck with the basic web.

After Ted Kennedy's Web site debuted, the Clinton administration introduced a full-blown site in October 1994 that included links to cabinet departments and other key federal agencies. A year later, seventy-year-old John Warner, chairman of the Senate Rules and Administration Committee, announced the creation of a Senate Web site, with links to a Web home page for every senator. By

December 1995, seventy-eight House members had Web sites.

No one in Washington seemed to doubt that the Internet would be a factor in the 1996 election. Why else would the Clinton campaign spend over $200,000 to design and maintain its site, which not only had position papers, speech texts, and economic growth charts but also had a handy device to allow users to contribute money by typing in their credit card number (this brought in about $10,000). The Dole campaign had a database of 70,000 supporters' E-mail addresses, which received specially tailored messages on a regular basis. Third-party candidates had Web sites. Special-interest groups and media organizations got in the game, too. It didn't hurt that once a site was up and running, the Internet was basically free.

So November 5, 1996, became the first big election night of the wired age. The Internet had only been a relatively obscure academic computer network in 1992. This time around, up-to-the-minute voting results would be reported. CNN and *Time* magazine collaborated for AllPolitics. MSNBC, the effort from NBC and Microsoft, was up. CBS put out Campaign '96. *The Washington Post*, ABC News, and the *National Journal* offered PoliticsNow.

But, as the first big election night of the wired age, all the Internet's weaknesses were on display. AllPolitics got so crowded that many people couldn't even get on. Instead of brightly colored electoral maps and detailed exit-poll data, they saw a comet flashing on their screens. That was AllPolitics' symbol that meant they were orbiting their destination. Modems crashed. Screens stuck. Then again, most of the people who used the Internet to get election-night results had been on it before. These problems were old hat.

Postelection polls found that 10 to 12 percent of voters—over 10 million people—had used the political Web sites. This seems dwarfed by the 60 percent who cited television and newspapers as their primary sources. But then, at a point when 20 percent of the

A NEW KIND OF PARTY ANIMAL

country uses the Internet (40 percent of 18–35s, the highest of any age group), the medium reached one in eleven voters. In the cryptic language of pollsters and consultants, this qualifies it as a viable means of political communication. Right now the Internet is used mostly by well-educated, higher-income Americans. The average Internet user is a twenty-seven-year-old college-educated white-collar worker earning more than $50,000 a year.

But it would be an enormous mistake to write off the Net as a tool of the elite. Internet usage polls are as varied as the medium itself—from defining an Internet user, to dealing with the multiple points of access, to the rapid growth of the technology. People who do not subscribe to a service or even own a computer can still use public access terminals at schools or even libraries. A study of the Public Electronic Network in Santa Monica, California, found that 25 percent of regular users log on from public terminals. When the Flatbush branch of the Brooklyn Public Library got hooked up to the Internet as a result of a $3 million grant, nearly 8,000 people in three and a half months signed up for half-hour sessions on the computers. In this low-income immigrant neighborhood, its streets lined with mango and plantain stalls painted the brilliant colors of the tropics, so many people waited each morning at the library doors that staffers taped down green stripes to indicate a line for patrons to wait in until one of a dozen computers opened up. As the technology becomes more widely available and less expensive (one of the Flatbush users, a twenty-year-old Haitian, ended up building his own PC after finding a Web site that showed him how to construct one), usage is expected to increase to 50 percent or more by 2000, when the largest potential voting-age bloc of all will be the one that is the most wired.

The television revolution took eleven years. When it first came out in 1949, less than 2 percent of households had a set. By 1960, almost 100 percent of American households had one. Compare that to the onset of E-mail. In 1993, E-mail was, at best, an intraoffice tool. Two years later, it had become a communications necessity. A business card now showed three essential things: a telephone number, a fax number, and an E-mail address. In 1996, 42 departments and agencies within the federal government spent $190 million on an estimated 4,300 Web sites and 215 computer bulletin boards. This was more than three times the amount spent in 1994, the first year the Web gained widespread popularity. Nearly one third of federal employees have Internet access, and 1.7 million have E-mail accounts. Yes, the computer revolution is well under way, a fact that has not escaped Ralph Reed and his army of social conservatives. "Computers are no more moral or evil than a spoon," says novelist Douglas Coupland. But modern technology can appear rife with peril. It gives exposure—and then, often, cohesion—to many different groups, which makes it more difficult for one preacher to reach the nation, or for one set of morals to become the accepted standard. This would present a problem to an organization bent on healing the fractured values of the nation. Quietly, at least initially, the Christian Coalition set out to do something about this.

———

"I am absolutely convinced that our approach will prevail," Ralph Reed told the reporter. He was referring to the Communications Decency Act, which outlawed dirty words on the Internet, and he had no reason to think otherwise. After all, legislators had consulted with the Christian Coalition while writing it (which prompted critics like *New York Times* columnist Anthony Lewis to snap that the bill would "limit speech [on the Internet] to what Pat Robertson and Ralph Reed approve," or, "reducing all users to the level of children"). Brushing aside any censorship concerns like so many annoying gnats, Reed knew that he could rally enough votes in Congress to pass it, and that President Clinton, heavy into his final campaign, had already indicated that he would sign it. Oh, there were a few rumblings about what the courts might do if the legislation ended up in their jurisdiction, but for now Reed didn't so much as bat his pale blue eyes.

He had the waxy face of a missionary, and the serene smile he flashed at television cameras disguised a politically astute mind. Before Reed took over as the executive director of the coalition, he had been the executive director of the College Republican National Committee, and the founder and executive director of Students for America, a group for conservative college students that Reed built to a membership of 10,000, with chapters on 200 campuses in 41 states. By the time he got to the Christian Coalition in 1989, very few people of any age could boast the organizational skills he had.

The coalition had been founded by Pat Robertson after his 1988 presidential campaign, with the aim of "helping Christians have an effect on the political process." That was what the Internet site said, anyway. One of the first things that Reed did was start a donor file. "Once people realized he was the guy with the money, he became the guy they all called," said a twenty-nine-year-old Republican operative. "He doled it out with a grin to local groups across the country and basically got them to bury any petty differences and rally around a larger agenda." That took a knack for networking and an abundance of charisma. But Reed's most vital bit of knowledge was how to use religious fervor to his advantage. "Listen, Ralph Reed and about a quarter of the coalition know the hot buttons to push," said a young consultant who has worked with the group. "They know how to get these people to open their checkbooks and call the 900 numbers."

Reed also had the right look, which enabled him to accomplish the impossible: He made the Christian right seem friendly, especially after dour Pat Robertson and blow-dried Jerry Falwell. Reed rarely lost his temper in public, an invaluable asset in an age dominated by the unblinking television camera. As an editorial writer at the *Wall Street Journal* said, "It doesn't matter what you say on television. People only remember what you wore." A member of the most media-savvy generation would realize this.

Under Reed, the Christian Coalition became a force of 1.9 million members, and saw its budget leap from $200,000 in 1989 to $27 million by 1997. During the 1996 election, the organization distributed 45 million voter guides in 125,000 churches. But what brought the Christian Coalition off the fringe and into mainstream politics was Reed's strategy of economic instead of values-based arguments. After all, not everyone has the same values, but everybody has the same currency. The $500 child tax credit seized on so stridently by politicians of every ideology did not originate with the coalition, but Reed made sure that his organization took the issue as its own. This was not, Reed said, "a Christian agenda, Republican agenda or special interest agenda—it's a pro-family agenda." And to the coalition, the Internet most decidedly did not fall into the category of "pro-family."

The organization threw itself into the campaign to censor the Internet. In Congress, in the Supreme Court, and on the grassroots level (this last one assisted by that patron saint of propriety, Donna Rice) the freewheeling environment of the World Wide Web came under attack. In the spring of 1996, just as Reed had expected, the Communications Decency Act sailed through Congress. Members railed on the House floor about the need to protect children from pornography on the Internet. Many of the same congressmen had never even typed on a computer keyboard in their lives, let alone taken the leap into cyberspace. They had no idea how difficult it was to find pornography on the Internet. I overheard one congressman in the halls of Longworth, telling another that "sometimes, if you leave a computer on and go out to dinner, you come back and there's pictures of naked women on

*A NEW KIND OF PARTY ANIMAL*

your screen!" His colleague nodded in solemn agreement while I bit back what I wanted to say—*"That's a helluva computer, sir!"*

The four-term southern congressman who was the driving force behind the initial bill wasn't much better. He came late to the debate. The Communications Act of 1995, which overhauled the telecommunications industry, had already passed out of the Commerce Committee and was scheduled for a vote on the House floor. The congressman, who had a near-perfect record of voting with the Christian Coalition, called his top aide from the Capitol. "I want to get in on the action," he told her.

"But you're not on the Commerce Committee," she said.

"I don't care," he persisted. "Find me an issue."

The aide came up with an anti-child-pornography bill. And that was how a congressman who had never been on the Internet and who didn't even have a computer in his office became the arbitrator of technology decency. The issue got snapped up by the Republican leadership and eventually evolved into the Communications Decency Act, which made it a federal crime to put on-line—where children might see it—not just the obscene or the pornographic but any "indecent" word or image. "Some way, somehow," growled Republican Senator Charles Grassley of Iowa, "we will have to find a constitutional way of protecting kids from porn." He, too, was not known for his on-line prowess.

The ignorance is real. A surprising exception was the Supreme Court, which did accept, after all, a case questioning the constitutionality of the CDA. During arguments about the act, the justices displayed considerable computer literacy, a highlight coming when Antonin Scalia pointed out that technology is changing so rapidly that what is constitutional today could be unconstitutional next week.

Young people already regarded politicians who attacked the Internet as suspicious. The minds behind legislation like the Communications Decency Act hardly improved on that. When people who don't know the first thing about a new technology presume to make laws restricting that technology, they tread on the dangerous ground of threatening their own validity. The machine behind the act was something different entirely. The people who participated in that knew exactly what they were doing, prodded on by Ralph Reed's efforts. Their track record was strong. Just months after first taking office, Bill Clinton had attempted to lift the ban on the use of Medicaid funds to pay for abortions. The Christian Coalition had zeroed in on fifty-two members to persuade into seeing things its way. By using radio ads, phone banks, and massive mail drops, the organization contacted over 250,000 households in key congressional districts. In the end, the House voted to maintain the ban. Forty-three of the fifty-two targeted members voted with the Christian Coalition. Pat Robertson had envisioned success like this just four years after he'd founded the organization. On election night in 1992, as Robertson got ready to be interviewed by Tom Brokaw, Reed whispered in his ear, "Be prepared for him to ask whether we are trying to take over the Republican Party."

"What is left to take over?" Robertson replied.

---

The Communications Decency Act provided Ralph Reed with the perfect opportunity to influence policy, this time around from a values-based argument that was sure to work in an era of new and deeply felt insecurities among older Americans. In changing times, Americans historically have clung to virtues that make them feel safe. While flappers and hepcats read a new type of novel, *This Side of Paradise* by F. Scott Fitzgerald, their parents revisited a more familiar and seemingly genteel period in Edith Wharton's books. But with technology bringing about changes that are more rapid and intrusive than ever, adults project their fears on to their children in an old way but with a new twist.

The 18–35s were used to being on the receiving end of the insecurity of older Americans. A "self-absorbed, spoiled, directionless lot, whose ephemeral attention spans and rueful ignorance of the political process will effectively leave the nation without an intellectual or philosophical anchor," as a *Vanity Fair* reader put it in 1996. But that was nothing compared to the hostility that older Americans were feeling toward the under-seventeens. In 1997, a survey by the policy research group Public Agenda found an unprecedented level of generational disapproval that extended beyond teenagers. Over 50 percent of adults offered negative descriptions of children from age *five* to seventeen. "My daughter is wild," a Denver mother told researchers. "She is seven going on twenty-one." Nearly half thought that children from five to twelve were spoiled and unappreciative, and six out of ten adults believed that these children would not make the United States a better place, or would even make it worse. Feeding directly into a values argument, the hysteria surrounding the alleged impending self-destruction of children reached new heights of the ridiculous. When a 1996 RAND Institute poll asked older Americans how likely they thought it was that they would be attacked by juveniles, they said a one-in-four chance. Since youth offenders primarily victimize each other, this fear was largely unfounded. Senior citizens stood a better chance of slipping in the bathtub. But why ruin a good scare? Even the federal government fell for it, pouring $11 million into a gang-prevention program (overheard between two elderly women in Chicago: "Kids without values join gangs"). One such session was held for seventh graders in trim and tidy Manassas, a suburb of Washington, D.C. When a reporter asked the gang data analyst at the local police department if the city had seen any indication of gangs at the school, the officer replied, "We had some activity a while back, but I can't recall anything around the middle school. Wait. I remember a fight in the schoolyard a few years ago, but lately it's been quiet. Maybe the guy moved out or graduated or left the school or something." The seventh-grade teacher added, "We have no gang problem. But there may be potential. We have to do proactive work." So how did out-of-control brats, ripe for gang recruitment and crime, get that way? Over 50 percent of adults cited a "lack of values."

Ah, yes, values. In an election year, both Democratic and Republican politicians grasped at values as the answer. To cite this as a solution was easy. More difficult was the actual follow-up. But why let reality ruin a good line? Older Americans were more than willing to embrace the pitch, and virtue became hip. A spate of books about values was written from every political perspective, from *Democracy's Discontent* by liberal Michael Sandel to *The Book of Virtues* by conservative Bill Bennett to *Values Matter Most* by middle-of-the-road Ben Wattenberg. At campaign stops, Bill Clinton promised to "protect our values." Bob Dole said he would resurrect "old values." In the world of entertainment and culture, the public-relations executive who used to represent Michael Jackson began promoting the concept of a "Statue of Responsibility" as the Southern California counterpart to the Statue of Liberty. Actor Charlie Sheen, who spent $50,000 in one year on Hollywood call girls, declared himself a born-again Christian (less than a year later, he would plead no contest to allegations that he beat up a former lover). Talk-show sleaze king Geraldo Rivera, who on one episode had fat sucked from his rear end and injected into his forehead, now claimed he was going to clean up his act, saying, "I'm sick of the garbage that is on [daytime television]." A moral recovery seemed well under way.

But, when the people who make up the bulk of social conservatives were children, their culture consisted of radio and comics. Religion, education, and family sifted through information and entertainment and decided what was "appropriate, thus forming firm boundaries." Today, those boundaries are as watertight as a sieve. Children are techno-savvy and well-equipped as they sit amid cable channels, videos, faxes, cellular phones, and, of course, the Internet. It was and remains naive for people to buy into the social conservative's argument that the Internet can be controlled. First of all, the Internet was born during the Cold War, envisioned as a way of decentralizing communications to make it less vulnerable to attack. Second, if the mullahs couldn't keep the bikini-clad actresses in *Baywatch* off Iranian TV, how did social conservatives expect to manipulate an infinitely more nebulous medium like the Internet? All the talk about virtuous virtual reality only served to make older Americans look completely out of touch in their children's eyes. Kids didn't need Bill Bennett's pithy tales of plucky pets to grow up with a sense of morality. But, the latter was an easy solution compared to the proactive reality.

"One of the functions of parents is monitoring—you monitor their homework, their friends, what they're really doing in their spare time," said a developmental psychologist at Columbia University. "I don't think we've said enough about how the demands on parents change when early adolescence hits. . . . Monitoring is critical." But since "monitoring" took so much "quality time," parents preferred to rely on other methods, like censorship, to protect and promote values.

And what, precisely, are these values? "Respect for elders" is one, although the same adults who believe that—and over 80 percent do—might not be able to grasp the arrogance of asking children, whom they do not respect, to nevertheless have respect for them. Of course, no one ever said that impudence does not increase with age. So, it was not startling at all that older Americans who overwhelmingly believe that children are trouble are also wary of the power and freedom offered by the Internet.

What the Christian Coalition does not realize, and what many older Americans choose to ignore, is that attempts at controlling "decency" standards violate the basic premise of the Internet culture: that information should be free and uncensored. "Decency" standards and blocking software like Net Nanny, so popular with parents right now, only give an illusion of control. Politicians and parents lull themselves into complacency with these. Meanwhile, 18–35s and the children coming up behind them will get around the standards and the software as quickly as they can type. The twenty-first-century version of Thomas Paine's pamphlets has arrived, whether or not social conservatives and older Americans are comfortable with it.

———

Kim sat in the studio under the bright glare of camera lights. Between television and radio quips, Kim's friends would tell her they couldn't turn anywhere on election night without hearing her voice. *Ahhhhh!* she thought, gleefully appalled, *I'm a spokesidiot!* KCOP, the Universal affiliate in Los Angeles, had tracked her down through the voter guide and arranged for her to be their Internet correspondent that night.

"And now, Kim Alexander will show us a few of the chat sites that are happening this evening," the anchorman said.

They were live as Kim clicked on the Yahoo! site. She had shown the CNN site in her previous segment, so she wanted to do something different. But then, just as the camera zoomed in, the screen went bright pink, and up flashed: ARE YOU A LESBIAN?

"Uh, Kim, remember, this is a live, *family*, TV audience," the anchor said gruffly, clearing his throat.

"I pulled up an ad," Kim said. "Sorry."

The crew, of course, started laughing as soon as they broke to commercial. Kim grinned and shook her head. And her grandmother was watching this, over in West L.A.!

Election night was almost over. The Internet did a fine job of covering that in its first go-round. Twenty-six percent of voters were regular users. This would only increase as the technology got easier to use and less expensive. Before the election, during her final public demonstration of the California Voter Foundation guide, Kim had handed out lists of public libraries throughout the state that offered Internet access. It wasn't going to be so exclusive the next time around. And in at least two California races for U.S. congressional seats, Internet sites had a role in unseating the incumbents. Both Walter Capps and Ellen Tauscher had Web pages up early in their campaigns against, respectively, Andrea Seastrand and Bill Baker, who did not have sites. When the challengers won, their managers credited the Internet with putting them ahead.

And the CVF Voter Guide had 30,000 log-ins and 200,000 accesses. Some of the users even sent Kim personal messages: "I was totally confused by all the garbage ads and literature, and your site gave me a place where I could read the facts and decide for myself"; "I'll be a very informed voter this year"; "I think this is what the Net is all about."

As for electronic filing, she certainly put the fix on the state legislature. Kim's interns, armed with laptops, practically lived in the secretary of state's office for two weeks. They never wanted to see the inside of that place again. But it paid off. *The Wall Street Journal* rated the Late Contribution Watch project as one of the "Best of the Best" Web sites, and now the legislators themselves were beginning to capitulate. All signs pointed toward electronic filing becoming law in the next session. The representatives figured it was inevitable, anyway. No doubt, Kim had single-handedly kept the issue alive. People in the mainstream "old" press admitted that much—privately. Because CVF listed late campaign contributions, and because Kim made sure that hundreds of journalists received regular E-mail updates, dozens of newspapers ran articles on their state representatives. "By telling the story," Kim said, "you keep a story alive." She couldn't help but feel a surge of hope. She'd won! She'd won! She'd won!

The point of no return had been crossed. The CVF guide

linked up to 140 campaign sites, all of which had not been used to attack opponents but to make the case for why the candidates should be elected. That was progress. "We're all going to have to step out of the roles we play every day and look at what we're doing in the electoral process," she told her friends.

The Internet was virgin territory. Everyone made up the rules as they went along, just like in the early days of radio when people struggled to write, produce, and speak for the new medium. The biggest challenge Kim faced was cutting through it all. So much information, so few hours in the day. And then, one day, the phone rang.

"This is Geoffrey Smith," the man said. "I'm a political science professor at UC Davis. I think we can work together."

Around this time, Ralph Reed announced that he was leaving the Christian Coalition. He had spent the pivotal years between ages twenty-seven and thirty-five with the organization, and found that its nonprofit status was "very restrictive." His decision came as the Federal Election Commission was examining whether the Christian Coalition had abused its tax-exempt status by directly supporting Republican candidates. The coalition's chief financial officer would resign over the issue. Reed denied any wrongdoing and decided to start a campaign consulting firm. He called it Century Strategies and said he wanted to create a "farm team" of hundreds of "pro-family, pro-life, pro-free enterprise" candidates at every level of government—local, state, and federal. Reed did not rule out running for office himself.

"He will be able to earn fabulous sums as a political consultant now that he is going back to his roots, which are as a political activist, not an evangelical," sniped one critic. Moderate Republicans in Congress privately admitted that they were relieved—few had forgotten the Reed-driven full-court press on abortion, school prayer, or Internet censorship.

Later, a former one-term congressman from Washington State,

Randy Tate, would be named Reed's successor as executive director. It was a move eerily similar to the Sierra Club's appointment in 1996 of a twenty-three-year-old as president, and, like the environmental group, the Christian Coalition admittedly was hoping Tate's age would attract young people into its ranks. Tate didn't exactly look younger than his predecessor. For starters, Reed had hair. But the fact remained that, at thirty-one, Tate *was* younger than Reed, even if he could not have discerned the Foo Fighters from Chinese food (Tate's nickname, "Rockin' Randy," was coined by a fellow congressman to poke fun at his innate lack of musical hipness). The coalition was banking on the age factor, tempering the appointment by announcing Tate would be sharing duties with a sixty-two-year-old. Not surprisingly, none of this offered encouragement to young people that the organization remotely understood them.

A coast away from Reed's press conference about his departure, Kim was on a roll. On her way back to Sacramento from Davis, she shook her head in disbelief almost the entire way. She couldn't get over the irony. For the past few years, she had been trying so hard to make her ideas reality, and she had never considered the possibility that there were other people out there just like her. It wasn't like she ran into support groups at cocktail parties. But there were a lot of other people, who thought the same way as Kim. Professor Geoffrey Smith was one of them. He had been teaching students how to create Web pages for the past year, and while cruising the Internet he saw her proposal for a comprehensive legislative guide. Kim had been putting all her proposals online for the past year, hoping that someone might run across them and say, "How can I help?"

She struck a partnership with Smith. His students at UC Davis would build sites for the CVF legislative guide, designing it to help people with everything from the California lawmaking process to directions to the capitol. They would also put together a database of the voting records of legislators—which numbered upward of 6,000 bills at any given time—and ratings by interest groups. Kim had had this in her head a year ago. Now, she had an army of ninety students to work on it. A guide like this did not exist on paper. A guide like this didn't exist *anywhere,* but in a few months it would be real! "We are just going to burn through content," she murmured aloud.

*Information is power.* And she was going to empower people. The biggest obstacle to interaction was that people were so damn busy. If they were going to know what was going on, information needed to be easily accessible and timely. This guide would be up by 1998. And then let's see if California doesn't get more responsive and accountable, Kim thought. It was all so delicious.

A few months later, the Supreme Court would raise her spirits even higher when it overturned the Communications Decency Act on the grounds that the law "threatens to torch a large segment of the Internet community." Justice John Paul Stevens would write, "Through the use of chat rooms, any person with a phone line can become a town crier with a voice that resonates further than it could from any soapbox." The Christian Coalition would call this "frustrating" and "a sad day for our nation." The Clinton administration would announce that it would immediately conduct a brainstorming session to develop an Internet equivalent of the television V chip. But, the ruling would mostly give a booster shot of hope to an age group that had grown up with the Internet and with the overwhelming opinion that any interaction with the government could only conclude adversarially. The system, in a refreshing way, would work.

It would be some of the validation that Kim had longed for. And she would think back to the day she'd first explained her idea for a legislative guide to a lobbyist. The man had interrupted with, "Don't you think you're instilling a sense of hope that's only going to be quashed?" Kim's jaw had dropped. *Oh, I don't think so,* was what she wanted to retort. But the thought that politics had been turned into a horrible, ignoble mess momentarily stunned her. It could be better. It would be better. And as she drove toward Sacramento under the brilliant blue sky, she pressed her lips together with conviction.

## Chapter Six

# YEAR OF THE WOMAN

*In politics, women . . . type the letters, lick the stamps,
distribute the pamphlets and get out the vote.
Men get elected.*

—Clare Boothe Luce,
congresswoman and publisher

Lynn Marquis called Robert George two weeks after the 1996 conventions. Washington still soaked in the late summer heat as sparks of fireflies flickered through the evenings. The resigned tranquility was almost unsettling. Four years before, the city had been tense with anticipation—of a victory, for the Democrats; of a fight, for the Republicans. But this time around, the presidential campaign had already lost its luster, even in the politics-mad capital ("This is unnatural to the point of weird," noted columnist and

Washington veteran Meg Greenfield). Congressional staffers yawned through the speeches and focused only fleetingly on the races that affected their employment. Sloths with bunions moved faster than this election season. Still, most politicos didn't think beyond it. As usual, their focus went cycle by cycle. So Robert was mildly surprised when Lynn asked, "What do you think of 2000?"

"It's supposed to be a good year," he answered. "Why?"

"I'm thinking about running for office. You know, maybe for the state legislature and build toward Congress," she said. And before Robert could ask why she was calling him, the opposition, Lynn added, "I'd do it as a Republican."

Washingtonians, young and old, loved to play the who-will-run game. It didn't matter what race. In winding hallways and airless rooms, over pear martinis at Ozio's or Stoli Dolis at the Capitol Grille, the question was bantered about. This was the main industry in a place where people picked who ran for what office, which candidates got how much money to do it, and what the party platforms would be. So a congressional staffer who expressed a serious interest in running had the luck of accessibility to the right people. That was what had happened six years before when Blanche Lambert Lincoln decided to run for the First District of Arkansas. She had worked on the Hill in the early 1980s for that district's congressman, Bill Alexander, before taking a job as a lobbyist. By 1991, when Lincoln was twenty-nine, she thought the federal budget was out of control ("Wait a minute," she told friends, "when I couldn't pay my phone bill my last year of college, I had to sell my stereo. Why don't these people get their act together?") and that nobody was *moving*. Her father had always said, "Don't complain unless you're willing to do something about it." Lambert Lincoln went back to Arkansas and told him she was going to run for Congress. "Blanche," he said, "I never meant for you to take me so literally."

Lambert Lincoln ran against her former boss in the Democratic primary. Senator David Pryor advised her to have fun. "If you don't, people won't like you," he warned, "and if they don't like you, they won't vote for you." She had a blast. With her mother, she whipped up a buffet table of barbecued brisket and potato salad for her first press conference. "Reporters have to eat, don't they?" Mrs. Lambert said when her daughter's Washington-based political consultant shook his head in bewilderment. Reporters loved attending Lambert Lincoln's press conferences. And Lambert Lincoln went out and told her fellow Arkansans what she would do in Congress, all with a sweet-tea voice and eyes that snapped with intelligence. "Blanche is so smart and so good at what she does, I'd work for her for free," a leading consultant said. She beat the pants off Bill Alexander in the primary and went on to win the general election.

Not everyone who came to work on the Hill wanted to come back as a member, but a lot of them did. Some succeeded. Trent Lott from Mississippi went from congressional chief of staff to congressman to senator. Lyndon Johnson had been a staffer. So had Robert Kennedy. On and on and on.

Staffers had the advantage of knowing exactly what the job entailed. They understood they would be working up to eighteen hours a day with no time off on the weekends—that was reserved for returning to their districts and their constituents. They understood they would give up their private lives, and that everything they said and did would be scrutinized by the media.

"You don't win unless you have the money, and you don't get the money unless you're taken seriously," Robert said, and he would know. He had spent five years at the Republican National Committee, observing those decisions. And frankly, despite the success of a few female politicians, he didn't see the old guard losing sleep over the campaign ambitions of any female staffers. Young male staffers were a different story, historically speaking. If the parties thought you had the spark and the stomach for the long, often painful haul to office, then they groomed you and assisted you. More young women than ever before might be working on Capitol Hill and in senior staff positions, but the establishment boys' network remained so firmly secured that female staffers kept a semi-serious list of the "Top Ten Members You Don't Want to Be Alone in an Elevator With."

Now, *that* was how the old guard worked. Robert didn't think that way—hell, he was part of a very large group of young Republicans who wondered why Elizabeth was not the Dole on the presidential ticket. The question they asked wasn't, "Can a woman do the job?" The 18–35s in the staffer ranks asked, "*Who* can do the job and do it *right?*" It was fine and well for Robert and his fellow Washingtonians to subscribe to this—even critical, since they soon would be the "guard" itself. But for it to become a reality, their peers in the electorate also would have to believe. And as Robert began to explain this to Lynn over the phone, a press assistant handed him the results of a poll.

"Lynn," he said as he scanned it, "I've got something you should see."

It was another campaign poll, one of hundreds in number-nutty Washington. It asked the usual questions, including, "Do you think more women should hold political office?" More than 84 percent of 18–35s had answered yes, over a third higher response than any other age group. One poll was one poll. Robert did media. He knew it didn't *really* count unless the numbers came up at least twice. He pulled open his file drawer and yanked out a manila folder. And there it was, in another poll: 84 percent of 18–35s thought more women should run for office (the pollsters themselves had noticed this, too; "What this means," one noted privately, "is that the usual gender bias line is gone, at least in politics. They will elect the first woman president, and she's probably even going to come from this age group"). Over fifty years after the Nineteenth Amendment gave women the right to vote and twelve years after Geraldine Ferraro became the first woman to run for vice president on a major party ticket, the gender shift had finally happened. But, for all it noticed, the establishment might have been hit on the head with a Styrofoam frying pan.

Then again, it could have been a lead frying pan and it wouldn't have mattered. Today's elderly grew up on the heels of women's suffrage, which, many were taught, was the same as communism. There had been one flicker of hope in their childhood. During the 1936 Democratic National Convention, Molly Dewson, the director of the Women's Division of the National Democratic Party, managed to get a female alternate appointed to every position on the platform committee. Each woman stood ready to attend every meeting, which forced the men into a first-ever record of perfect attendance. Otherwise, they faced a platform written by women. It was, as *The New York Times* proclaimed, the "biggest coup in years." But, just like a lit match, this advancement was snuffed out quickly. To the children and teenagers of that era, a female politician remained an oxymoron. And, by and large, they raised their children to believe this and more. Agnes E. Meyer, an author and humanitarian, observed in 1962 that "if a young girl happens to be intelligent, she is made to think that she cannot afford to be a 'brain' lest she scare away men of less intelligence." Meyer proved to be of her time because the only way she could imagine women in power was through the state of motherhood. The women of the world would unite to protest the Cold War, she wrote, telling their leaders that "we, as the mothers of the race, emphatically object." A Harvard professor would write three years afterward, "As far as I can judge, 'leading' women are all too often inclined to lead in too volatile, moralistic or sharp a manner." This generation was firmly in charge of both political parties in the late 1960s when former vice chairman of the Democratic National Committee, India Edwards, said, "If the party backs a woman [for office], you can be sure they do it because they think it's a lost cause but they know

*Year of the Woman*

they have *some* candidate" (the chairman of the Democratic National Party himself cheerfully admitted, "The only time to run a woman is when things look so bad that your only chance is to do something dramatic").

The mothers of the housework-in-high-heels era (even though a 1955 *New York Times* headline warned "Housework Is the Road to Boredom") would regard, with shock and horror, the actions of their daughters in the late 1960s and early 1970s. They nearly choked on their own virulence at such a seemingly passé trend as not wearing a bra. "If I've had to wear a bra all my life," one snapped to a reporter in 1970, "why can't she?" Many even cited bralessness as justification for the killing of four Kent State University students by the National Guard. Two of the victims were female. This atmosphere wasn't exactly conducive to erasing gender barriers. And, in fact, despite the advances of the feminist movement in those years, the boomers remained stymied by this aspect. In 1973, a then-aspiring professor heard her peers, "those male college seniors running to meet job recruiters with their button-down shirts and sober self-importance," perfunctorily dismiss her ambitions: "You'll end up just a housewife, anyway"; "Do you want to be a ball-busting career woman?" She wryly observed, "To be a woman . . . was to have your Phi Beta Kappa key remarked on as if it was a novel charm bracelet."

Newspapers ran classified ad columns headed "Help Wanted, Male." On Capitol Hill, congresswomen were so rare that members didn't know whether to call Martha Griffiths, the architect of the Equal Rights Amendment, "gentle lady" or "gentlewoman" when they referred to their male colleagues as "gentlemen" (for the record, they decided on "gentlewoman"). When boomers predicted the future contributions women would make to politics, they expected their congresswomen to stick to tender, empathetic issues of the home, like child care and food programs. Mim Kelber, an author and legislative staffer to then-Congresswoman Bella Abzug, wrote an essay in the early 1970s about the year 2000, when "women in politics are old hat"; she foresaw a female president and a female secretary of state, except only after a nuclear holocaust.

The 18–35s came *after* the equal rights marches of the 1970s, *The Feminine Mystique,* and Bella Abzug and her hats. A woman had been nominated for vice president in 1984. One of the most visible leaders throughout the 1980s was Britain's Margaret Thatcher. Between 1974 and 1994, the number of female candidates for state and national office had more than doubled. So 18–35s didn't get held up by gender. When Madeleine Albright became the first woman secretary of state, young staffers paused instead at her age. "You know, she's got the Cold War mentality," mused a twenty-three-year-old legislative aide. "How's that going to flex with the 'global village'?" Even Pat Schroeder's weepy campaign rally in 1987 seemed ancient now. When the Colorado congresswoman cried on her husband's shoulder as she announced her decision to drop out of the presidential race, to older Americans, she instantly became a symbol of the stereotypical sobbing female. It was declared a disaster for the future of women running for Congress. Less than ten years later, there were 236 women running, and empathy was considered hip with the over-thirty-five crowd ("I feel your pain," said Bill Clinton). Nobody under thirty-five cared whether or not pols cried. "It's all an act, anyway," sighed Lynn Marquis.

For young people today, the ability to lead was not considered exclusive to one gender. So when Lynn declared her intention to run for office, especially now with the electorate data proving that for the first time, for an entire age group there was no gender bias in politics, it carried just as much weight as it would have had she been a man. Maybe more, thought Robert, since she was sharper than most.

"Let me get you a few phone numbers," he said, and he flipped through his Rolodex.

*Year of the Woman*

In December 1992, the Capitol Hill Women's Political Caucus popped champagne corks during a victory party for the "Year of the Woman." At long last, it had finally happened, nearly thirty years after Maine's Margaret Chase Smith, the first female senator elected without having been previously appointed and the first female senator to hold a position in the leadership (she was the chairwoman of the Senate Republican Conference), remarked that there were two main reasons more women had not been elected: "One—men, and two—women. Men because they vigorously oppose women's holding office, and women because they haven't stood together and exercised their majority voting power." Now, there were new images that emerged—like Patty Murray, the new senator from Washington, the "Mom in Tennis Shoes," and Cynthia McKinney, a new congresswoman from Georgia, the "African-American Mom in Gold Tennis Shoes"—who were camera ready. Many of the women publicly stated they ran in reaction to Anita Hill's treatment by the all-white, all-male Senate Judiciary Committee during confirmation hearings for Clarence Thomas. Of course, a couple of months later, every female senator initially would turn down seats on the judiciary committee, an ironic conclusion to their visceral reaction (after much cajoling by chairman Joe Biden, Dianne Feinstein would finally accept).

That night, though, the room fairly tingled with glee as Eleanor Clift, the crack campaign correspondent for *Newsweek*, was asked, "When will we see a woman elected president?" Eleanor paused briefly before answering, "I'm convinced we'll see her in our lifetime, but whoever she is, we don't know her yet. It'll be someone who's twenty-two, who's starting out now, who's inspired by what happened this year." But once the 103rd Congress kicked off, it became rapidly apparent that the so-called Year of the Woman was hardly going to inspire legions of young women to run for office.

The original modern feminists, the ones who had founded the National Organization of Women in 1967 and marched for equal pay, blamed this on "young women whose opportunities are the direct result of feminist efforts over the past three decades [who] are generally unwilling—or too uninformed—to acknowledge that debt." At least, that was how feminist pioneer and author Sheila Tobias put it. Tobias and her peers had hiked down a long road. Remembering the not-so-long-ago days of a conference of women state legislators that she attended in 1972 at Rutgers University's Center for American Women in Politics, Tobias said, "I recall a legislator from the Midwest bemoaning the fact that she found it necessary to print her campaign literature on the backs of recipe cards, the kind housewives could file. . . . Another legislator, well into her sixties and obviously experienced and talented, was forced . . . to give up her seat in the Georgia state house when her husband became a stroke victim [because] her constituents fully expected her to be at his side. . . . There they were, older on average by twenty years than their male colleagues because for the women, state office was a mid- to late-life prize for decades of volunteering. For their male associates, the state house was supposed to be a stepping stone to higher office."

And now, twenty years later, California sent two women to the United States Senate: Dianne Feinstein, who went on to distinguish herself by flip-flopping on high-profile issues like the balanced budget whenever it seemed beneficial; and Barbara Boxer, who had the intellectual impact of a cream pie (during the Persian Gulf War, Boxer, then a congresswoman, went to the House floor and recited, singsong, the Bette Midler hit "Wind Beneath My Wings"). Illinois sent Carol Moseley-Braun, who promptly became embroiled in a campaign fund scandal. On the House side, Eddie Bernice Johnson from Texas became infamous for dismissing a staffer who was pregnant. And a seven-term veteran, Barbara-Rose Collins from Michigan, distinguished herself by becoming the first member of Congress to have her staffers file discrimination suits against her. At the turn of the nineteenth century, suffragists had maintained that society would improve with the fairer sex at the helm. "Pure in spirit, selfless in motivation and dedicated to the preservation of human life," recorded historian William Chafe, "women voters would remake society and turn government away from war and corruption." Others, like Edward K. Bok, the editor in 1909 of *The Ladies' Home Journal* (all irony of that aside), decided after sifting through "hundreds of letters from women who are deeply interested in [the suffrage issue]" that " . . . the average American woman is too busy [to vote]. Take the average wife or mother who has, say, two or three children and a home of her own. She likes her books, she is fond of music, she may have a taste for pictures. That woman is busy . . . you cannot interest her in extraneous subjects because there are too many things of a vital nature that are distinctly woman's own questions."

Neither prediction fully came to pass. Despite Bok's condescending assessment, women did find the time to vote, although they did not bring about the expected peace that Chafe remarked upon. And, as it ended up, female politicians, in general, had no moral superiority over their male counterparts. An ego was still an ego. So the theory that the elderly grew up with—that women leaders are an anomaly—had been disproved. The theory that the boomers espoused—that women would be kinder, more empathetic politicians—had been shattered. All that remained was the question asked by 18–35s: *Who can do the job right?*

And young people had a vaguely empty feeling about the women in the 103rd Congress. As a congressional force, these women had not panned out. The real power in Congress belongs to groups that band together over common issues. When the freshmen Republican class of 1994 stood together on the Contract with America, their solidarity became infamous. They nearly brought down the Balanced Budget Amendment when the

Gingrich-approved legislation did not include a two-thirds majority vote to increase taxes. That had been one of the planks of the Contract. Only a last-minute deal to bring up the issue separately quieted them—and even then, grudgingly. "They just don't care if they're reelected or not," said one veteran Republican congressman. "They truly believe they were sent here by the voters on a mission."

The women who won in 1992 did not form such a caucus. They tried, at first. With Pat Schroeder chairing the women's caucus, they emphasized abortion rights, protection against sexual harassment, women's health, and family leave. But not every female member of Congress was consumed with these issues, which left veterans like Schroeder with a bitter taste. "They're not leading for women," she said of Susan Molinari and Deborah Pryce, who were Republicans. And some wanted to concentrate on other things. Blanche Lambert Lincoln, for one, focused on restructuring Superfund, which tried to eradicate hazardous waste sites, and on fiscal responsibility.

"Listen, I care about women's and children's issues," Lambert Lincoln says, "but there were other issues, too. I had been in Washington before. I knew exactly what my ideas were and how I wanted to go about implementing them. Women need to respect each other for the choices they make." Lambert Lincoln's situation had been crystallized two years earlier by a women's history professor, quoted in the book *Professing Feminism:* "There has to be respect for other people's decisions to live certain kinds of lives, whether it's to have children or not to have children, to be married to men or not to be married to men. These choices can't be seen as excluding someone from being a thoroughgoing feminist."

The larger debate, simmering under the surface and stoked mostly by women legislators who had broken the path for others, was: What, exactly, made a "proper" political woman? For groups like EMILY's List and the National Organization of Women, the answer was simple: women with pro-choice, pro-family agendas. Clinton advisor Ann Lewis called this the 1996 campaign's "*Redbook* strategy," and under this standard even Republicans admitted that "for the time being, the Democrats hold all the gender cards" (a twenty-nine-year-old staffer at the Republican National Committee put it more bluntly: "We don't have a gender gap; we have a gender *gulf*"). In response, well-educated, well-connected conservative women started their own ideological group, the Independent Women's Forum. With 550 dues-paying members and 1,500 on their mailing list, the IWF published a newsletter and various opinion pieces. "That's no white male, that's my husband," they liked to say. Susan Faludi, author of *Backlash*, deemed them "pod feminists" who practiced "no-risk feminism for a fearful age: just post your achievements, make nice with men and call it a day." If Faludi's cohorts regarded young women as "unwilling" and "uninformed," the IWF had a take on them, too. The organization offered the press a letter, written by a middle-aged woman. She described young women in this way: "They engage in sex indiscriminately and have abortions without remorse. I want to cry when I think of what the future holds for them."

So, depending on which theory 18–35s bought into, young women, including those who are politically inclined, are either shortchanged or face lives of wantonness. It is a bewildering choice presented by the women who went first—and who don't want anyone to forget that. The Third Wave Direct Action Corporation, a feminist group for young women launched in 1992 by then-twenty-two-year-old Rebecca Walker, has been criticized by older women as "unfocused" for an agenda that includes racism, pollution, and poverty. When Vanessa Kirsch, the twenty-six-year-old founder of the community action group Public Allies, asked at a meeting of older feminists what bits of wisdom they would like to pass on to younger activists, one replied, "Say thank you." The room burst into applause. In account after account, stacking up like war stories of old, eighteen- to thirty-five-year-old women are brushed aside by veterans who say, "I'm not dead yet," or, "That's my issue; I've been working on it for twenty years."

Outside the established feminist movement, young Americans moved on. Their reality had been shaped by a new culture of working mothers who were either trying to stretch the family budget or were hard on the career track. Between 1960 and 1980, the proportion of mothers with children five and under who worked at full- or part-time jobs rose from 20 to 47 percent. Throughout the 1970s, the number of latchkey kids under the age of fourteen, left alone after school, doubled. So, many 18–35s grew up helping around the house in ways that their parents never did as children. A news report in 1956 had the headline, "A Scientist Looks at Suburbanites—Species Is Found Centered on Child and Home with Mother the Chauffeur." By comparison, over 36 percent of 18–35s even cooked their own dinners. As a result, they were not wracked by the same dilemmas. In 1996, less than 31 percent of men in their first year of college thought women should stay home with their children. In 1967, fully two-thirds of men agreed. Interestingly, in 1958, 80 percent of female students in high school and college insisted their place was in the home, while slightly more than half of their male colleagues agreed.

When it came to politics for today's young people, the gender package didn't matter. Capability was what counted. Whether Sheila Tobias's peers grasped this or not hardly mattered to 18–35s. They had already revamped the rules.

———

"You can teach 'em to type," former Texas congressman "Good Time" Charlie Wilson used to say, "but you can't teach 'em to grow tits." (This from a man who actually had an impressive profeminist voting record.) Ah, the old days, back when Joe Morgan divided women staffers into two categories: those he wanted in his bed, and those who had turned him down, also known as "bitches." Ah, the new era, in which there was a remarkable number of bitches on the Hill ("I would call them 'smart,'" Lynn said). "Anyone who doesn't get that things have changed," a thirty-year-old legislative director once commented, "is going to have to leave."

When Bob and Lynn came to the Hill in 1992, women were overrepresented in clerical jobs in the House by 15 percent. Within four years, that had declined to 8 percent and women made up 38 percent of the leadership positions—chiefs of staff, legislative directors, press secretaries, and district directors. Despite the television impression of Washington as a sea of wrinkled white-male faces, women occupied a higher percentage of top positions in congressional offices than they did in other sectors of the U.S. economy. The pay gap had also narrowed. In 1996, for the first time, there was not a statistically significant difference in the salaries of men and women in the House. More 18–35s than ever worked for women in positions of power—or alongside them—and made the same amount, whether male or female.

The Joe Morgans and Charlie Wilsons were leaving, which eventually put me in an unprecedented situation when in 1993 a writer from *The Washington Post* approached me about a story idea. "I want to talk to you every few weeks about your experiences, coming to Capitol Hill, how people treat you as a woman," he said. "Then, I'll write an article about it at the end of the year."

It was flattering to be asked, especially after wallowing in unemployment for three months, but since I had no intention of reentering those ranks—and because my new boss probably wouldn't be too enthusiastic about his communications director getting press for herself faster than for him—I turned down the offer. Still, about every fifteen months, the writer would check in:

"How are you treated as a woman in that environment?" I had no answer for him, other than, "Uh, fine." Gone were the days when congressmen would chase staffers around desks. Because of the Congressional Accountability Act of 1995, aides could press charges. Besides, it wasn't as if sexual harassment didn't have other consequences. As Bob Packwood found out, the ever-hungry media was just a phone call away.

Frustrated and stymied, the writer finally asked, "Is there a story here at *all?*"

I didn't hesitate. "No."

So, not surprisingly, it wasn't the "Year of the Woman" that inspired Lynn to run. It was her own congressman, when he gave her the brush-off. Because he served on the same committees as her boss, she saw him all the time. Always, she greeted him with: "Hi, Congressman!" Always, he never so much as glanced at her in acknowledgment. At first, Lynn thought he was just preoccupied. But her boss, Bill Brewster, grinned at everybody. It was in his character—Bill Brewster genuinely liked people and enjoyed chatting them up. And a member of Congress never knew when he would run in to a constituent. Even the briefest meeting could mean a vote. So the next time Jim Moran stormed past Lynn, she thought, "Wait a minute—I *am* a constituent of his."

When she wrote to him about the need to solve the Medicare crisis, he didn't write back for two months. Bill Brewster had a two-week turnaround time for letters. "I could do the job better than Jim Moran," she thought. And the more she considered this, the more she thought, "Forget Jim Moran—I could do the job better than most of the people up here."

She mentioned to Bill Brewster that she was thinking about running. She didn't say for what office or against which candidate. If he thought she could do it, that she would be good at it, he would be supportive. Members of Congress didn't have to encourage their staffers to run on their own. The only issue of loyalty in a congressional office was the staff's to the congressman, not vice versa. So when Bill Brewster's face, usually twinkling good-naturedly, creased with seriousness, Lynn was taken aback.

"If you run," he said, "I'll be the first to contribute to your campaign."

Tears nearly sprang to her eyes. Lynn had not expected this. "Even if I run as a Republican?" she asked.

"Especially if you're running as a Republican," he said, and the grin returned. "Why would you run as a Republican?"

Lynn had thought this out. If you were considering a run for public office, the first step was usually to side with one party. This was not a brain stumper in the old days. Most aspiring politicians knew who they identified with. But now, it wasn't quite so clear. Lynn didn't think she would make a very good Democratic congresswoman, not when she would be expected to back an unbalanced budget and ignore entitlements. The social policies of the GOP didn't thrill her, either, but she wasn't going to be about abortion or school prayer. There were bigger, more vital issues. Lynn would have felt it to be more accurate to run as an independent, but she also wanted to win. A candidate needed money to win, and at this point in time independents notoriously came up short. Just like Jerry Morrison, Lynn knew what she stood for. She wanted to balance the budget, responsibly and for real. None of this "off-the-table" crap for her, which was what most members did with tender subjects like Social Security and Medicare. That wasn't the philosophy dished out by the majority of the Democratic Party, and after the welfare and Medicare battles of 1995 (and the reprise in 1996), the lies, the spinning, the put-your-finger-to-the-wind mentality of politicking, Lynn was left exhausted and sapped of faith. That, at least in the 104th Congress, was the life of a Blue Dog. Bill Brewster belonged to this caucus, a group of about twenty-two Democrats who were fiscally conservative.

"We came up with the idea on a hunting trip," said Blanche

*A NEW KIND OF PARTY ANIMAL*

Lambert Lincoln. "We were sitting on a back porch, talking about how our ideas were good and gelled with the folks outside Washington. The only way for us to be effective was to band together. And you know, when it came down to budget and welfare reform, we *were.*" The Blue Dogs came from every part of the country ("A Blue Dog is a Yellow Dog who's held his breath," joked Texas Congressman Ralph Hall, distinguishing this group from the Yellow Dogs of the early 1980s, a group that had consisted of southern conservative Democrats, both men and women). They were immediately taken seriously. Minority Leader Richard Gephardt met regularly with them and brought their welfare and budget legislation to the House floor for a vote—in the 103rd Congress, that rarely ever happened—and the Republican leadership appointed them to conference committees. But because several Blue Dogs eventually switched from the Democratic to the Republican party, the group was also immediately regarded with suspicion by more liberal members. Two-term Democrat Cynthia McKinney sneeringly deemed them "Newtnicks." When Blue Dog staffers tried to attend the Democratic Caucus meetings, where the party's political agenda was discussed, they were asked to leave. "We don't want you passing on our secrets to the Republicans," snapped a liberal congressman. In the most partisan Congress in eighty-five years, it certainly did not help when their own party beat up on them.

This would not improve in 1997, when William Weld, the extremely popular Republican governor of Massachusetts, was nominated by Bill Clinton to be ambassador to Mexico. Weld, a libertarian when it came to social issues, had never endeared himself to the socially conservative wing of his party. Massachusetts voters might love his independent streak, but Jesse Helms most certainly did not. *He* happened to be the entrenched senator from North Carolina, the chairman of the Foreign Affairs Committee, and damn sure against allowing a vote to approve that fool Yankee to take place on the Senate floor. Few Republican senators rallied to Weld's cause. His nomination was killed by the hand of his own party. "In plain language," Weld said, "I am not Senator Helms' kind of Republican. I do not pass his litmus test on social policy, nor do I want to." But, Bill Weld, a fiscal conservative and social independent, was the future. Jesse Helms, a bitter old man who was one of the last vestiges of segregation, must have looked at Weld and felt fear. His day was over, and he knew it.

In the meantime, as Lynn saw things, the moderate forces in the Republican Party needed people like her. And then Bob asked the hundred-thousand-dollar question: Where? Of course, he asked only after laughing maniacally and shouting, "You'd run as *what?*"

"Don't get too carried away," Lynn said. "I'd run as a pro-choice Republican."

"Who cares!" Bob exclaimed. "You'd be running as a Republican!"

"Now, wait a minute," she said. "I've got some very good reasons. . . . "

Bob wasn't listening. She could have said she agreed with the way Gingrich cut his hair, for all Bob cared. He was going to dine on this for months!—years!—decades! However long it took her to actually run.

"So," he said, "where will you run?"

The general political assumption was that one ran in her home district, like Blanche Lambert Lincoln did. But precious few 18–35s were going to fit that standard, when they were the most transient age group of all. In Lynn's case, she lived in Virginia, although she was a native of New England, and to top it off, after her year with Bill Brewster, she spoke with an Oklahoma accent, especially when she talked about crime ("Line 'em up and gun 'em down!"). The parties had been known to pick seats for their up-and-comers. But, as long as the ardent conservatives remained strong in the Republican primaries, there wasn't much chance of that happening for Lynn.

A NEW KIND OF PARTY ANIMAL

"You need to figure out what you believe in and run in a district that has the same concerns," Quinten Dockerty told her one evening. Quinten was an old friend by Washington standards, since Lynn had known him for three years. He was also one of the names that Robert had pulled out of his Rolodex. They had worked at the Republican National Committee together. At thirty, Quinten had spent over six years at the RNC, distinguishing himself when he walked out of a family values meeting with the Christian Coalition's Ralph Reed. "I knew what the guy was going to say," Quinten said later, shrugging. This did nothing to diminish his stature with the committee. He even weathered the melodramatic "you-weren't-there-in-the-wandering-years" proclamations from forty-year-old veterans. Quinten knew his stuff after identifying potential donors and raising money for several successful congressional and senatorial campaigns.

"If you're going to attack Social Security and Medicare," Quinten said, "you're not going to do well in south-central Florida or on Long Island. Demographics are everything. Frankly, that's what Newt did. He moved from Louisiana to Georgia to teach at a college that suited his beliefs a lot better.

"Most important of all," Quinten continued, "you need to know why you're running. The worst thing in the world is a candidate who doesn't know why he wants to be elected. That was Bob Dole's problem. He could get the machine together, but he couldn't answer why he should be president. That's what ruined Ted Kennedy's campaign in 1980. Roger Mudd asked him, flat out, on television, and he had no answer. It's not just about the race. You need the passion and the drive, and you need to be willing to lose at least once." He smiled wryly.

"I don't want to lose," Lynn said quickly.

"Nobody wants to lose," Quinten replied. "But it's a rite of passage you may not be able to avoid. You need all sorts of things to win, and one of those is name recognition."

Lynn knew deep down that the odds were lousy that she would make an immediate leap from staffer to member. And, to boot, every peer who had been elected recently was part of a family dynasty—Patrick Kennedy, Jesse Jackson Jr., Harold Ford Jr. Lynn didn't have to *start* with a U.S. congressional race. She was realistic enough to know that she'd probably be more effective at the state level, especially with the current trend of transferring federal programs to the states. But she also knew that unlike the political scions, she embodied the emerging new politics of the 18–35s. Not only did she walk and talk the nonpartisan line, she put high stock in her beliefs, and stuck with them. She owed nothing to a machine and thought that truth was the best marketing.

Quinten was privately relieved that Lynn was interested at all. The GOP needed faces other than Ralph Reed and the hip, young, conservative women who seemed to be trotted out for every television camera. A "cause that less resembles a battle, than, let's say, a cocktail party," was how the *Weekly Standard* described them. Quinten didn't have a problem with smart women wearing miniskirts. It was the fact that they marketed this trait so assiduously, landing on the cover of *The New York Times Magazine* and in glossy photo spreads everywhere, that made this seem like in-your-face compensation. See—*we have women here, too!*, the diametric opposite of the jowly, lumbering white-male mainstay, wearing their gender as a badge as much as their NOW counterparts on the Democrats' side.

"No matter where I run," Lynn said, "I'll need a lot of help."

"Candidates always do," Quinten said. He grinned. "Name the time and the place."

———

In August 1995, artist Ann Moliver Ruben, who had designed a T-shirt that read "Someday a Woman Will Be President," was told by a Wal-Mart buyer that the message "goes against Wal-Mart's family values." Wal-Mart yanked the T-shirts from its shelves in Miramar, California, just outside a Marine base, after two customers complained that the message "was of a political nature that they didn't agree with," according to Jay Allen, vice president of corporate affairs. Less than four weeks later, the shirt was back, the result of a national uproar. Allen admitted, "We made a mistake."

Two years later, psychologists like Barbara Mackoff were pondering how today's parents could nurture their daughters into becoming leaders. "We have to urge them to honor what they think and feel; I call that 'making her the authority about her experiences,'" said the Seattle practitioner. This wasn't much beyond the summation that little girls commonly heard when Mackoff was growing up. Twenty years ago, author Peggy Lamson observed, "It must be very difficult indeed for a young woman to visualize herself in the role of a politician. Little girls do not dream of growing up to be Governor; women's fantasies do not carry them into the realm of public office."

By 1997, this wouldn't be a sentiment shared by only girls. When Senator Susan Collins of Maine visited an elementary school, she asked the seventy-five students gathered in the multi-purpose room, "Do any of you boys and girls want to be politicians when you grow up?" Not one hand went up. For today's children, envisioning themselves in public office is hampered by a new set of difficulties that go beyond and do not include gender. This transformation began with the 18–35s, while older Americans remained stuck in perceptions that had been honed in their childhoods. For the 18–35s on down, the question of gender in politics became a nonissue. It happened so obviously, yet in such subtle waves, that young Americans took it for granted, while their elders didn't pick up on it at all.

Consider that when 18–35s grew into their college years in the late 1980s, women not only outnumbered men in graduate school but also received 55 percent of bachelors' degrees, 53 percent of masters' degrees, and almost 40 percent of doctorates. Ten years ago, women earned about 45 percent of bachelors' and masters' degrees and less than 30 percent of doctorates. When young Americans entered the workforce, many ended up with female bosses. In the past decade, the number of female executive vice presidents more than doubled and the number of female senior vice presidents increased by 75 percent. Women own 7.7 million businesses in the country, employing 15.5 million people and generating $1.4 trillion in sales. And, firms owned by women—which are growing more rapidly than the overall economy—are more likely to have remained in business over the past three years than the average U.S. firm. This is vastly different from 1955 when author Sloan Wilson wrote, "There's happiness as money in marriage, girls!"

With advancements in education and business, opportunities for women are expected now. Feminist pioneers like Sheila Tobias would point out that this is a luxurious position, hard-won by others. But this is called progress. It is not a lack of respect or an appreciation of the moment. In every other aspect of politics, 18–35s question authenticity and capability; why would anyone expect that "gender" would be different?

And, unlike twenty years ago, when the ideology of female politicians was almost entirely liberal, now there are plenty of options to choose from. Although a preponderance of women in the House would still be classified as liberal Democrats, there are also conservative Democrats like Pat Danner of Missouri; conservative Republicans like Jennifer Dunn of Washington; moderate Republicans like Connie Morella of Maryland (whose conservative detractors snidely referred to her as "Commie" Morella); and just about every nuance in between. Such a variety fits with the inclination of 18–35s to vote based on specific issues.

For young Americans, support of women politicians is not simply a sweeping generality; it comes down to the individual herself.

Barbara Kennelly, a Democratic congresswoman from Connecticut, is admired for her integrity and her stance on issues of financial equality. And then, on the opposite side, the disdain among the Wicker Park set for Senator Carol Moseley-Braun is not because she is female. "She lied, she cheated, and she let us down," says Greg Gillam. "She's exactly what I can't stand about politics." And Greg had passed out campaign literature for Moseley-Braun in 1992.

As the standards of 18–35s pass into the mainstream (midway through the 1996 election, after young Americans' tendency to vote based on issues received some press coverage, pollsters noticed that thirty-six- to forty-nine-year-olds were starting to cite "issues" as their main criteria for voting), women who are seeking office will be held to the same requirements as men who are seeking office. At a time in which both parties have already been found to be seriously flawed, so too have women politicians been found to be just as fallible as men—as well as just as capable.

———

In New York, a nine-year-old girl was overheard asking her mother, "Who's Diana Ross?" She pointed to a bus ad for Diana Ross's new album. "She's one of the original Supremes," her mother replied.

"Cool!" the little girl exclaimed. "Even before Sandra Day O'Connor?"

Things had changed, all right. And considering it was now a given among eighteen- to thirty-five-year-olds that women were politicians, both successful ones and otherwise, and that young women had just as good a shot at office as young men, then there was nothing startling about the expectation among 18–35s that any politico their age—male or female—had to break a new path.

"What we have to realize," Kim Alexander said, "is that no one's going to change politics for us. The people who're in charge have no reason to want to change it—why should they? They know how to make it work for them. We have to do it ourselves, and right now there's a huge opportunity to create something different that can stand on its own."

She meant, of course, having young people run Internet campaigns. This is how Kim figured her peers could break into politics at a fairly early age. Most of the time, youth worked against political hopefuls. When Patrick Kennedy, at the age of twenty-seven, ran for U.S. Congress in Rhode Island, he got slammed by the media for "wanting to be our congressboy," despite the fact that he had already racked up more time in the state legislature than most U.S. congressmen. And Patrick Kennedy had the name behind him, too.

"Cyber campaigns," Kim said. "If young people are going to win, this'll be how."

She thought that Lynn would need about $10,000 to put up a Web site and get her ideas on-line. From that base, media appearances and position papers could be listed and links to other sites could be built. "Think about it: Most people are never even *asked* to vote," Kim pointed out. "People vote for you if they think they know you and know your ideas. Here's the tool that does that, and does it quickly and inexpensively."

Jerry Morrison had told Lynn pretty much the same thing when she met with him during the Democratic convention. He was waiting for her when she walked into Urbis Orbis, a loftlike coffeehouse in Wicker Park, with scraped wooden floors and stacks of dusty magazines and newspapers. Most of the customers wore flannel shirts and had some body part pierced. Jerry stood out in a blazer and slacks.

"Don't get the wrong idea," he told Lynn. "I only look like this because of the convention."

He ordered tea—which Lynn found a bit charming, this burly man with the union pin on his lapel stirring the delicate brown leaves in his cup. Then he looked her in the eye and said, "So you want to run. Well, I don't know where you're thinking about doing it, but the one thing that matters is that people feel they know who you are. They want to know what you believe in. The way I did it was registering people to vote. If you register twenty thousand, you're good for seven thousand to actually turn out. In a multi-candidate race, that'd really shake things up. You'd get the established party scared. They'd have to deal with you."

He took a sip. "So what would you run as, anyway?"

Lynn sighed. She never would escape this question from her peers or the comment that usually followed.

"A pro-choice Republican?" Jerry smiled. "Good luck."

Yeah, yeah. Lynn rolled her eyes and tried to laugh. Despite the fact that she tripped along the same abortion line that the majority of her peers did (as in, "Government shouldn't be involved in personal matters"), she knew there were rumblings that after the 1996 election the GOP would take up the issue of partial-birth abortion and use that to chip away at *Roe v. Wade*. As a rule, Lynn did not get snagged in the abortion debate. The boomer-led antiabortion forces certainly didn't feel that way. They embodied their generation in that they liked nothing better than to argue morals and, every year, to send pro-choice members of Congress bouquets of blood-red roses that had been poisoned so that the flowers would die within a day. Lynn had spent the past two years triumphantly saving the roses by putting a little sugar in the vase and frequently changing the water.

"The problem," Lynn began, "is that it's so damn hard to run as an independent and win."

"Tell me about it." Jerry laughed, not unkindly. He told her about Chicago, the strength of the Democratic machine, the precincts, voter suppression, and the 1999 race for alderman.

"But don't you sometimes feel," Lynn began, "like you're fighting a losing battle?"

Jerry shrugged. "Abraham Lincoln lost eight or nine races before he won anything," he said. "There are too many people here who feel the same way I do for me not to have an impact."

This went beyond Chicago, down to North Carolina, where Charles McKinney thought the same way. "I'm not the only one under the impression that both parties have sold out," he said. "I know that there's people who want to run for office who think the same thing. So why don't they take the chance that we'll be there? They can't take what happened to Ross Perot after '92 as the norm. Who among us wanted Ross Perot to have his finger near the Button? Just once I want to see someone stand up and say, 'This is what I believe in. You might not agree, and this might not be the popular thing to say, but let me give you my reasons. If you elect me I will stick to these principles.'"

And so the questions echoed: *Who* can do the job? *Who* can do it well? *Who* cares about gender? Another notch clicked on the geared clock wheels as the future ticked closer.

Jerry Morrison raised his cup at Lynn. "To 1999 and 2000," he said.

"And beyond," Lynn replied.

# Chapter Seven

# *PARTY ON*

### ATTENTION GEORGETOWN STUDENTS!

**IF** you register to vote in D.C., you will become a legal resident of D.C.
1. You must pay D.C. income tax.
2. You may lose any grant money from your home state.
3. You must obtain a D.C. driver's license.
4. You must register your car in D.C. and any Zone 2 parking sticker you now have would be revoked.

It wasn't the first shot, but it was the proverbial one heard 'round—well, maybe not the world, but at least the U.S. courts. Westy Byrd, a middle-aged Washington matron, had always been irritated by the students at Georgetown University. It was the classic, ongoing battle between colleges and communities: Citizens felt that students were overrunning their neighborhoods and students felt that they should have some rights as a result of bringing their economic base to the area. In this instance, Westy Byrd summoned up all her righteous indignation against a student-led voting registration drive, Campaign Georgetown, when she "anonymously" wrote the flier. As the chairman of the Advisory Neighborhood Commission in Georgetown, she felt correct to the core of her being when she told reporters, "I don't hate students, but when residents who don't live here vote, the vote of the residents who do live here becomes meaningless."

With her pushed-out front teeth and pinched nose, Westy Byrd looked just like her name. She probably never imagined that the small sheets of paper stuffed under dormitory doors would have exactly the opposite effect that she had intended. Students flocked to the Rock the Vote table at the university center as the Georgetown campaign brought together nearly every element of the real youth movement in politics. It was local. Its strategy focused on high voter turnout. It did not concentrate on party affiliation but on specific issues. And, it ignored any preconceived glass ceiling in politics, not seeing "young women" and "elected officials" as mutually exclusive terms. It did not include an Internet element, but that was because, Campaign Georgetown president Dan Leistikow said, "We had the luxury of being able to meet everyone face-to-face. Otherwise, we would've had something up on the Web." And, of course, it shook up the establishment with the sophistication of its understanding of politics.

One thing the students definitely understood was that as long as they had no representation on Georgetown's Advisory Neighborhood Commission, they would be at the mercy of people like Westy Byrd. Before 1990, it wasn't unusual for students to get elected to one of eight commissioner positions on the Georgetown ANC. Just about every neighborhood in Washington had an ANC, which served as an advisory board to city government. ANCs really were toothless tigers, but in their own way, the commissioners ruled the local streets. Student representation effectively ended when Westy Byrd cut the campus into puzzle pieces during redistricting.

Instead of the university encompassing one district, bits of it were scattered through six. Ever since, the Georgetown ANC had managed to stymie plans by the university to build a day care center and had prevented students from holding block parties.

So in the summer of 1996, twenty-one-year-old Dan Leistikow and about fifty other students decided to launch an effort to get 100 percent of the eligible voters on campus registered. They offered a choice between registration in home states (through the motor voter form) or in Washington, D.C. "We had no idea," Dan said, "that we were about to get into a six-month-long fight in the courts over this." Especially once Westy Byrd and other like-minded Georgetown residents found out that two students were planning to run for commissioner spots. Out went the flier, which Westy Byrd had paid for with ANC funds. When the students protested this as a form of voter intimidation, the chairwoman defended her actions in a letter to the D.C. Board of Elections and Ethics. "Recent voter registration of more than 900 Georgetown University students requires an immediate and thorough investigation," she declared, "to insure that all bona fide new residents have paid and are paying D.C. taxes and fees as required of all residents."

The chairman of the board, Ben Wilson, immediately corrected her. "It has long been established by the Courts that students have the right to register to vote in the jurisdiction where they attend school as long as they are not registered in any other state," he said in his reply. "It is erroneous to assert that as a precondition to voting, students must pay taxes or obtain a local driver's license . . . [and your letter] may be suggestive of voter intimidation."

And that was how everyone ended up in court, but only after Westy Byrd shot back to Chairman Wilson, "If you have any legal authority whatsoever for even intimating that my letter or flyers may 'be suggestive of voter intimidation,' I demand that you either apprise me of that authority immediately or formally retract your ill advised and libelous statement." After this exchange was publicized, to no one's surprise at Campaign Georgetown, students flocked to the voting booths. The wait was over two hours in some places. And the two students, James Fogerty and Rebecca Sinderbrand, won their races for commissioner. Who says every vote doesn't count? In Rebecca's race, her margin of victory was five votes. Their elections would be challenged by Westy Byrd and her allies, but in March 1997 the D.C. Court of Appeals would uphold the constitutional right of students to vote in the communities where they went to school. James Fogerty and Rebecca Sinderbrand were sworn in two hours before the first ANC meeting, during which Westy Byrd, although still a commissioner, pointedly was *not* reelected to serve as chairman.

"The fight wasn't about voting," Dan Leistikow said later. "The fight was about *principle*. We knew what we stood for, and we dug in our heels."

The students at Georgetown, and Jerry Morrison, Quillie Coath, Lynn Marquis, and Kim Alexander, are not isolated examples, scattershot across the country. They embody the majority of 18–35s. "We are not going away," Kim Alexander warns. "We're going to be around for a long, long time." The continuation of politics as we know it directly depends upon the faith and credence that up-and-comers give it. And, 18–35s are more than a bit unsure that the current system is the best, or even the most effective. Between the Democrats and the Republicans, there has been "decades of bad news," as Gary Hart has put it. In the 1970s, Richard Nixon resigned, congressmen tangled themselves in sex scandals, and Jimmy Carter implied that the country was suffering from a malaise, although much of this exists for 18–35s in the form of history books and documentary retrospectives. During the Senate campaign finance hearings in 1997, several journalism colleagues of mine excitedly recalled how they "rushed home from work to watch the Watergate hearings on TV." They were utterly surprised to learn that I hadn't watched them. "No," I said, "I was too busy learning how to walk." In the 1980s—more vividly recalled—Ronald Reagan and George Bush may or may not have been involved in arms deals with the Iranians to supply the Sandinistas in Nicaragua with funds; meanwhile, over 240 high-level appointees of both Reagan administrations were investigated or indicted for criminal or ethical misconduct; the savings and loan industry failed and needed to be bailed out by taxpayers; and thirty-two members of the House of Representatives lost their jobs after writing bad checks. The 1990s aren't even over, but already we have seen President Clinton implicated in a shady land deal and a sex scandal, both major parties may or may not have violated fund-raising laws, and CIA agent Aldrich Ames betrayed his coworkers and his country because of greed. And the major parties are astonished that 18–35s assiduously steer away from labels like "Democrat" and "Republican."

Distinctions that have been made for sixty years need to be reconsidered now. "Liberal," "conservative," "Democrat," and "Republican" aren't valid anymore. As the old terms become inapplicable, be prepared for variations of "independent." It has been applied to the politics, films, and social mores of young Americans to the extent that to be otherwise implies that someone or something is less than genuine. During the 1997 citywide primary elections in New York City, one under-forty city council member (who did admit that the writing plainly was on the wall as far as attracting young voters in order to remain in office) fiercely insisted he was not necessarily a Democrat. Instead, he was an *independent*. Whether or not the council member truly was an independent is another matter, and it is one that will become a common scenario for voters eighteen to thirty-five to sift through as politics continues to shift their way.

"Liberal" is associated with crumbling housing projects, holier-than-thou attitudes, and "wouldn't-it-be-great-if" theories. It is seen as tax and spend, a budget that is never balanced, and wasted handouts. It is seen as bloated bureaucracy, bully-pulpit reasoning, and blithe dismissals of the future to bankroll overgenerous programs today. "Liberal" is the lyrical cadences about racism delivered by the Reverend Jesse "New-York-Is-Hymietown" Jackson, the blue-collar labor leanings of Richard "So-I-Own-a-Huge-Beachhouse" Gephardt, and the severe definition of feminism by NOW president Patricia Ireland. But the heart of liberalism, to look out for the little guy and manifest social change, still remains. And there are many 18–35s who wholeheartedly believe in this. However, they do not necessarily buy into the strict interpretation of liberalism that seeks this change through legislation. For 18–35s, the leaders preaching this line already have an underlying image of disingenuousness. Young Americans who believe in making a difference socially trust in action through their communities. Instead of "liberal," call them, perhaps, "independent activists."

"Conservatism," at its best, is associated with a limited role for the government, and fiscal responsiblity. At worst, it means short-wave radio fanatics who are *convinced*, dammit, that black United Nations helicopters are sweeping the countryside, preparing to take over. It is seen as heartless attitudes, good ol' boys, and big business coziness. "Conservative" means the bombastic pronunciations of Dick "That's-Not-My-President" Armey, the cold insensitivity of Pat Buchanan, and the smug piousness of Pat Robertson. This impression prompts young people who do believe in economic conservatism (or, fiscal responsibility) to shy away from inclusion in these ranks. An important delineation: Those who are eighteen to thirty-five believe in this fiscal view in terms of economic *fairness*. For instance, 87 percent of 18–35s want to see substantial changes in Social Security, but almost as many also want to make sure that in the process the elderly are not impoverished. Borrowing a phrase from a Republican president who later ran as an independent, call them the "Square Dealers."

As for "Democrat" and "Republican," well, throw those labels out the proverbial window. The parties are headed for major changes, even if 18–35s have to drag them to it, kicking and screaming. Whether or not established politicos buy into all this is not the issue. Time is not on their side. Time is *always* on the side of the young. "Get it or get out of the way," said Kim Alexander. "We can work around you."

Over the past few years, the consultants, lobbyists, pollsters, elected officials, and bureaucrats who make up the mass known as "politics" have done their best to sell 18–35s the same package that they bought when they were young. Conservative pundit Irving Kristol has called it the "theory of the two Santa Clauses": Both parties have won voters and, in turn, elections by offering people goodies. First, today's senior citizens had the federally funded G.I. Bill for their college educations and then subsidized housing loans to suck them into the goodie system, and then they were kept there as they grew up and got older by the promise of Social Security and Medicare. It wasn't anything nearly so big that brought the boomers into the fold. For them, an ongoing series of tax breaks worked. Property taxes, capital gains, child and home school tax credits. And on and on it goes, promises here and deals there, as candidates create and feed this sense of entitlement. They do it because it works. In the film *The War Room*, candidate Clinton lambastes George Bush for making promises "he knows he can't keep, just to get elected." And then, without so much as an ironic wince, Clinton did the same. No age group—not the seniors, not the boomers—called them on this. That is, until politicians went to the 18–35s.

When they did, they encountered a group that regarded every word with suspicion. The candidates' replies during debates and press conferences sounded too smooth. *Did he say that*, wondered young people, *or did his PR guy?* No wonder the television audience dropped for the 1996 presidential debates. "Why should we watch it," Kim Alexander demanded, "when they barely answer the questions. They just say whatever their media consultants tell them to say." Ronald Reagan's mantra during the 1984 election was "the shining city on a hill." George Bush's in 1988 was "a thousand points of light." Bill Clinton's in 1996 was "we must build a bridge to the twenty-first century." These slippery images of the future swayed older Americans. But the young people, the very ones those words were supposed to be about, saw through the thick pitches. For every election in their memories, politicians had talked about "the future." The future, the future, the future. Repeat any word that often and it will be rendered as meaningless as the adjective "nice."

So, 18–35s came to view "the future" as something politicians said as filler, not because they truly believed it. To wit: Politicians like Reagan, Bush, and Clinton never actually *did* anything to help young people that went beyond window dressing. They might point to the war on drugs and National Service and say, "Look! That was for future generations!" In the meantime, Reagan declared ketchup a legal vegetable for school lunches and Clinton signed the bill that cut school lunches. All three regularly preached on the nebulous subject of "family values," but the sixteen-year-olds who ended up in Quillie Coath's P.R.O.U.D. program could tell them that a sense of family can't be *legislated*. In the thirty-five-year cycle of the oldest of this group, politicians have managed to accumulate a truly extraordinary track record of broken promises and empty rhetoric. And now they have the gall to wonder why young Americans barely stifle their laughter when they're approached by politicos with bright smiles and all the "right" words.

But, the politicians tried, all the same. They offered national health care (which young people would have subsidized for everyone else) and then they brought up college tuition breaks (which did not apply to students who were putting themselves through school). The 18–35s didn't bite. They weren't for sale, not in the

A NEW KIND OF PARTY ANIMAL

sense of their parents and grandparents, who had already bought into the system. Since health care and college tuition breaks seemed the best the establishment could do, it didn't look like 18–35s would ever swallow the dish. They would simply have to cook their own. This is exactly what made the players so uneasy. *We can work around you.* As politicians preach about "the future," the future has already arrived. The 18–35s are not on the outside looking in—they are on the inside, waving out at yesterday's establishment.

And so new rules are written. If politicians want to win in the future, they will have to change a few things. It will be something new and different for them to back up what they say, but general promises like "I am against crime" won't work. The Quillie Coaths and the Charles McKinneys will be right there, seeped in reality, to demand precisely what the candidates plan to do about crime, how they will pay for their plan, where that money is coming from, and why they believe what they say. When Representative Richard Gephardt went to New Hampshire in April 1997, ostensibly to recruit candidates for 1998 but more implicitly to lay the groundwork for a run at the White House in 2000, a state representative observed, "He is so afraid to say who he is. . . . He just tells us what the 'Families First' philosophy is, and I want to know why that matters to him." If Richard Gephardt—or any political hopeful—wants to win over the 18–35s, he must realize that he will be dealing with an electorate that grasps the link between local, state, and national governments. The Jerry Morrisons and Lynn Marquises will make sure of that. And the Bob Meaghers and Kim Alexanders will be there to ensure that politicians understand that their campaigns will rise or fall based on specific issues, not party affiliation or character.

Almost every politician who comes to Washington at least says he wants to change "politics as we know it." Then, of course, "politics as we know it" either changes the politician or the politician gives up and leaves town. The conservative Republican freshman class of 1994, the ones whom a veteran congressman observed "don't care if they're reelected or not," discovered after the 1996 election (and after some of them didn't come back) that their brand of take-no-prisoners politics wasn't working now that "moderation" was the new theme. To them, "compromise" was a swear word and "confrontational" was a compliment. Infinitely confident that victory was theirs in 1995, they had shut down the government twice during budget battles with the president. "The confidence grew from a belief that government was so unpopular that people would cheer," said the policy director of Empower America, a conservative advocacy group. "And, they didn't." Regardless of this, they attempted a well-publicized coup attempt to oust Speaker Gingrich in the summer of 1997 because, they felt, he had sold out his conservative beliefs in negotiating with the president. The coup didn't work, and it served only to make the rebels (as the Speaker's staff took to calling them) more zealously extreme than ever. "Some believed that they were especially anointed to define what the right course was for the party," said a Republican congressman from New York. And, a GOP pollster added, "The revolutionaries thought when they were elected that they were given Superman uniforms and they were impervious to pain. They're not."

Well, "politics as we know it," painful or not, *is* changing, with 70 million individuals driving it. If politicians want to stay in office, they will have to stick to their words, not change their policies based on popularity polls. However, they will have to carefully balance such integrity with compromise. Strict partisanship does not work. And as Charles McKinney said, "You've got to be doing something right if both conservatives and liberals aren't too keen on you." If young people give their commitment to a politician, they expect nothing less back. This demand for directness and for authenticity might be difficult for the old guard, seeped in poll dependency, spinning, and the goodie mentality.

By and large, this is how 18–35s regard the peers of Bill Clinton. In many ways, Clinton is the perfect president for this age of self-marketing. He does it on such a monumental scale that his election in 1992 was widely viewed as ushering in a new era of "baby-boomer" presidencies much in the way that John F. Kennedy began the G.I. presidencies. But as 18–35s come into their own in terms of the electorate and potential candidates, Clinton's cohorts might find themselves sidestepped if they don't get with the program. The oldest of the current eighteen- to thirty-five group will be forty-two in 2004, and, after all, the World War II generation decided to elect their first president when he was only forty-three.

That person could be someone like Blanche Lambert Lincoln, who maintains, "Change is good. Change is healthy. That's how you become inventive." She says this while changing her twin boys' diapers. She might not be the representative from the First District of Arkansas anymore, but Washington consultants still call her "the Natural." When she announced in the summer of 1997 that she would run for the seat of retiring senator Dale Bumpers, even experienced politicos were excited. "Blanche is the real thing," one says. "She's got moxie. She'll rock the boat. And she never cares if anyone laughs at her. She knows who she is."

Blanche Lambert Lincoln is one of the few established politicians who could capture the support of 18–35s. Just one year older than this group, she falls in the segment of the baby boom that identifies more with young people than with the generation that came of age over thirty years ago. When Lincoln refers to "people our age," she means the 18–35s. She has no use for partisanship. "I wasn't going to go to Washington afraid to challenge anyone, even my party," she says. "What good is that? I wanted to make it better." Lambert Lincoln didn't just shoot her mouth off about this. When she became a founding member of the Blue Dogs, she took some jibes from the liberals on the Hill. She didn't care. "I was honest and upfront," she says. "I did a good job. There's a certain amount of practicality in that."

Lincoln is an unusually young face for the Democrats. The party took the youth vote for granted in 1996, even after their '94 losses. They did nothing significant to curry favor or even show that they took young people seriously. Instead, they concentrated their efforts on blocs like senior citizens. This strategy worked in 1996, but at what cost? The Democrats are seen as the party of the elderly. The party's fund-raising base is even older than its membership. The inherent problem with this strategy is that its constituency will not be around much into the next century.

As for the Republicans, their economic stance is very much in line with a majority of 18–35s: Less is more. But, the GOP social policy—largely directed at this point by Christian Coalition conservatives—is almost completely opposite. Their insistence that the federal government should decide such issues as abortion and school prayer is not appealing. "As my late friend Paul Tsongas used to say, young people are in the great American center that's fiscally conservative and socially inclusive," observes Warren Rudman. The respected former senator from New Hampshire goes even further: "The Republican Party is making a terrible mistake if it appears to ally itself with the Christian right . . . the country is more centrist today than ever—particularly the younger generation."

When Rudman considered retiring in 1992 after serving two terms, he said, "The Republican Party I grew up with [was] the party of Eisenhower, Taft, Dirksen, and Baker, men who believed in a strong defense and less government, and who didn't think you could solve every problem by passing a law. If someone had told me in the 1960s that one day I would serve in a Republican Party that opposed abortion rights—which the Supreme Court had endorsed—advocated prayer in the schools, and talked about government-inspired 'family values,' I would have thought he was crazy."

Five years later, Rudman still feels this way. "The Republican Party is viewed by young people as being under the control of zealots," he says. "And if there's one thing young people aren't, it's zealots. They don't like the idea of people preaching to them." Among the attention-grabbing tactics by this segment of the GOP was the press conference in November 1995 denouncing former chairman of the Joint Chiefs of Staff Colin Powell and his possible presidential candidacy. And before, the same group had attacked Bob Dole's top Senate aide, Sheila Burke, as "Queen of the Senate" and as a "militant feminist." Not exactly the best image to put forth to independent-minded, non-gender-biased 18–35s. The taste will linger.

The wild card is a third party. But in the United States, where the political system is winner-takes-all, there is no room for three major parties. The most likely scenario is that one of the established two will fall and a new one will take its place. That has been the order of things since the nation's beginnings. From the Federalists and Anti-Federalists to the Whigs to the Know-Nothings to the Free Soil party, shifts have happened, and sometimes with critical results. After all, it was an upstart new party called the Republicans that in a matter of a few years produced Abraham Lincoln at a fairly important point in history.

And maybe that is what the Democratic and Republican parties fear today. In 1995, with independent sentiments running high and with 18–35s serving as the biggest resource for third-party petitions, legislators in fifteen states introduced bills to make it more difficult for independent or third-party candidates to get on the ballots. There was no need to tighten the law in Pennsylvania, where third-party candidates need 26,000 signatures to get on the ballot. A Democratic or Republican candidate needs 1,000 signatures. Still, the Pennsylvania legislature tried. It passed a bill in the final hours of its 1997 session that codified public office as the exclusive domain of Republicans and Democrats. Governor

Tom Ridge vetoed it. The Reform Party estimates that to run a national slate of candidates for the House, a new party will have to get more than 1.6 million signatures to meet state requirements— ten times more than a Democrat would need. The Libertarian Party estimates that to field a full slate of both federal and statewide candidates today, a third party would have needed 3.5 million valid petition signatures. In fact, ballot access laws in many states are so restrictive that they violate the 1990 document of the Copenhagen Meeting of the Helsinki Accords, the international human rights document that was signed by George Bush.

What most assuredly will *not* happen is a generational war, the oft-repeated warning that runs as an undercurrent through almost any argument involving age groups. The mostly boomer media has used it as a hook, and the so-called youth advocacy groups like Lead or Leave and Third Millennium have used it as a refrain. Lead or Leave's cofounders even drew up a possible scenario in their book: The U.S. has been crippled by a foreign power that has invaded "to darken our skies with toxic chemicals, infect hundreds of thousands of us with a deadly disease, plunge one-third of our children into poverty and homelessness, confiscate much of our income, and hollow out our cities and schools, turning them into war zones." All this "by the year 2000" because of a generational war kicked off by a $4.5 trillion national debt. Between the media and the youth pundits, "generational warfare" and all its sinister connotations have become a grenade with its pin pulled. Look out! It's going to explode! Soon! Not quite. The generations each can be (and are) guilty of thoughtlessness, greed, and arrogance. But *warfare* implies an unprecedented level of callousness and vicious- ness between child, parent, and grandparent. And, quite frankly, that type of ruthlessness simply does not exist.

Sure, the 18–35s may look at the boomers and senior citizens, and they may grumble about the former's dreamy idealism, obses- sion with values, and irritating self-absorption; and they may mutter about the latter's stubbornness, pious condescension, and blind you-owe-me attitude. And older Americans may look at these young up-and-comers and see cynicism, laziness, and superficiality (and they may wonder, as their elders before them did, "Oh no— *these* kids are our future? God help us!"). And each may point to the other, or even to everyone except themselves, as the culprit responsible for all the country's ills. But the fact is, this is just a hall of mirrors. Crack through a few panels and you find that the American generations consider it distinctly un-American to wish ill will upon each other. My former boss on Capitol Hill used to guide himself through the wilds of politics with two quotes. One he attached to his desk with Scotch tape. It was the reply that Benjamin Franklin gave to a woman who asked as he left the Consitutional Convention, "What kind of government do we have?" Franklin replied, "A republic, madam, if you can keep it." The second was from Thomas Jefferson, who said and assiduously believed, "It is incumbent on every generation to pay its own debt as it goes." It may be difficult to detect under the layers of rhetoric, media attention, and cynicism of today, but the words of Franklin and Jefferson embody the heart of Americans and their politics.

With more young people like Jerry Morrison running rogue campaigns on the local and state levels, and especially with the federal government empowering these levels by "downsizing," it isn't too off base to wonder if, instead of changing politics, 18–35s will eventually buy into *themselves* and, like every other age group, simply take over the system as it currently stands. For instance, just because young people don't believe in zero-sum politics as practiced by older Americans doesn't necessarily mean they won't develop their own brand of it. This would be a lot easier than overhauling everything. And maybe a case could be made for this—if it weren't for the inherent hesitation and generational diversity that makes us take a step back and observe. We saw the shattering results of politics as it has existed. And then, we got involved. "What we're doing," says Greg Gillam, "has no benefit for us unless we see it through to the end. We're not going to get a good résumé out of it. We're not going to meet Eddie Vedder. But we just might make a neighborhood we care about safe."

I left Capitol Hill after the "Republican Revolution," post-100 Days, and right before the conventions. Unlike Joe Morgan, who had quit under a veil of disillusionment, I brimmed with steely optimism. I might not have swallowed Bill Clinton's pitch for a "bridge to the twenty-first century," but I did not see "politics" as a decaying carcass, either. Well, sure there were a few worms. I seemed to know a lot of them. But during my last days on the Hill, several members approached me to say some variation of, "What is going on with you young people? We just don't know what you want anymore." I started grinning as soon as I heard this, and I couldn't stop. Because even as the politicians and the media decried me and my peers as cynical, apathetic, and uninvolved, I knew the reason why. *They hadn't figured out how to buy us yet, and this was driving them nuts.*

Our political psyche has already been stamped. Robert George might have thought the endgame was here, standing on Capitol Hill in the waning evening two years ago, but he was wrong. This is not the endgame. This is the opening move.

# Afterword

*Nobody can go to dinner here anymore without getting into a screaming match over Bill Clinton's sex life.*

—Maureen Dowd

Robert George fled to New York the night before the House voted to impeach the president. We immediately found a bar. Two sips into his beer, Robert put down his glass and demanded, "Can't we just kick all of them out? Republicans, Democrats, Clinton— everyone. Let's start fresh."

In a way, it was already happening. A scant month before, Minnesota had elected a Reform Party candidate ("a sideshow," Hillary Clinton had sniffed) as governor—just a day after the co-chairs of the Democratic and Republican national committees had argued on national television that though it might be nice to identify oneself as an "independent," ultimately Americans had to choose between the Democrats and the Republicans. The official reaction of the Washington establishment to Jesse Ventura's win was to dismiss it as a fluke resulting from the power of celebrity. After all, Ventura had been a professional wrestler, and the WWF did have better TV ratings than every political show combined. Considering the unusually high number of young voters, politicos collectively shook their heads. "This is what you young people do, waste your vote on a *wrestler*?" a Republican consultant asked me.

What made Washington uneasy was that Ventura's victory truly looked like the real bridge to the 21st century. Unlike his opponents, Ventura admitted he didn't have all the answers (he promised to learn what he didn't yet know). He specialized in straight talk, warning students, for example, that college loans might take a hit to help lower state taxes ("At least he admitted to it," a 21-year-old told reporters before casting his vote). He told Hillary Clinton, essentially, to stuff it.

Minnesota had the highest voter turnout of any state in the 1998 election, mostly because of Ventura. Exit polls show that most of his votes came from those under 40, and that 12 percent of all voters said they would not have participated if there hadn't been a good alternative. Seventeen percent of voters turned out due to Minnesota's same-day registration, and almost all of that vote went to Ventura, who won the three-way with 37 percent. "His strategy was to get more people to vote," points out Kim Alexander. After all, why squabble over the party stalwarts? When less than half of the country votes in a national election, money spent on the alienated could be a good investment for an independent. Minnesota had an active civic community on the Internet, too, led by Steve Clift of Minnesota E-Politics. Ventura took advantage of on-line debates and town hall meetings. "He didn't win because of the Internet," Kim says, "but he couldn't have won without it."

In a way it doesn't matter whether Ventura is a roaring success in the governor's mansion. He popped the Democrats' and Republicans' bubbles—just as Washington plunged into bitterness that outdid the partisanship of the Republican Revolution in 1995. The impeachment debate, already lurid by November, would become farcical: from the fanatic gleam in the eyes of Rep. Henry Hyde and his impeachment team (Bob Barr, a congressman from Georgia, looked straight out of central casting in his role as the Angry White Zealot) to the tit-for-tat revelations of adultery in the media (exactly who was being spun here—the politicos pitching the stories, the press who ran with it to make a reputation or a buck or two, or the public who seemed to want it all to disappear?).

The impeachment process would also become offensive. The president, who lied but was incapable of admitting it, deployed Stealth bombers over Baghdad the night before the House was scheduled to vote on impeachment. He said it was coincidence, but Americans of all ages—not just the cynical, media-savvy 18–35s—questioned his motives. The behavior of both parties as each vilified the other afterwards was ridiculous. In the end, the president has survived even if his reputation as an unprincipled, poll-following egotist is solidified, and Washington is in tatters. The policies of the Democrats and Republicans alike have become the politics of self-preservation.

If the co-chairs of their respective national committees remotely thought before the 1998 election that young people, who already leaned independent, would be brought into the parties as they grew up, they probably don't think so now. The Democrats and Republicans have virtually ensured that 18–35s will remain solidly independent, that the generation coming up behind them will, too (the National Association of Secretaries of State fretted when its 199 polling showed that over half of 14–21-year-olds regarded the major parties with disdain), and that older Americans will reexamine their concept of party politics.

Feminism has broken down, as well. NOW and other feminist leaders have asserted that what Clinton was accused of—having sex with Lewinsky and then lying under oath about it—isn't really bad. Betty Friedan added, "Even if he did what he is alleged to have done, what's the big deal?" Geraldine Ferraro has lobbied congresswomen on behalf of Clinton, arguing, "A man is a man is a man." The message seems to be: Clinton might be a dog, but he's our dog. As if there wasn't already acrimony between Second Wave feminists and younger women, the Lewinsky scandal has sealed it. That women who pioneered the concept of sexual harassment could swallow their own words is embarrassing and tragic. No matter how they've justified it ("But it was consensual!"), they sound like hypocrites, especially after hounding Senator Bob Packwood a few years earlier for much the same reason. While Blanche Lambert Lincoln became the youngest woman elected to the U.S. Senate in 1998, the women's movement defined by activists like Gloria Steinem was being consigned to history books.

Young people have not been completely unforgiving of the president, though. Ennui settled in among my peers. Other Americans might have seen the impeachment as another sad chapter in the last half of the century, but for us it was "business as usual." A scandal in the White House is nothing new. There was little the media could do when the story broke, even flashing catchy graphics ("Crisis in the White House") with ominous theme music, to gain our attention. We focused elsewhere: on our communities, as a 1998 study by the nonprofit Public Allies found; on the Internet, as Jesse Ventura discovered; and on the future. Clinton only had two years left in office. "He's like the elephant in a room," said a 26-year-old elementary teacher. "You ignore him and hope he goes away."

Many times over the last year I was asked by reporters and politicians alike, "is Monica Lewinsky emblematic of your generation?" I tried not to laugh, but it *was* funny. *Oh, yes, we're all Beverly Hills–raised twentysomethings with a father-figure complex.* They were still looking for a quick way to describe us. To them—sometimes even to us—we would always be young, dressed in flannel, and talking about our ideas. Lynn Marquis even used to joke, "Oh, we'll never be in charge." The future seemed far, far away. But then, in 1999, we woke up and found ourselves no longer the youngest, suddenly wearing suits, and a lot closer to leadership positions. "Well," Lynn said recently, "it *was* bound to happen."

# Notes

## Notes on Sources

I primarily drew my information from interviews. Many, including congressional staffers, members themselves, pollsters, and consultants, spoke on condition of anonymity. All persons and incidents portrayed are real, although in some instances certain identifying details are changed, and Joe Morgan, Quinten Dockerty, and Richard Heathers are pseudonyms. Bob Meagher, Lynn Marquis, Robert George, Charles McKinney, Quillie Coath Jr., Jerry Morrison, Greg Gillam, Roger Romanelli, and Kim Alexander, among others, offered their time and insights for the record. Kimberly Schuld, formerly of The Polling Company, Jefrey Pollock of Global Strategy Group, and Curtis Gans of the Center for the Study of the American Electorate were invaluable in translating numbers into theory.

## Introduction

11  "Shock, Horror": Reuters, September 1995.

12  "Our Muddled Youth": I. F. Marcosson, *American* magazine, September 1936, pp. 24–25.

12  "Youth Gone Loco": *Christian Century 55,* June 12, 1938.

12  "The Perpetual Youth Problem": N. M. Butler, *Vital Speeches of the Day II,* October 7, 1937, p. 24.

12  "sheep-like apathy": Maxine Davis, "Today's Lost Generation," *Literary Digest,* April 4, 1936.

12  "even now rotting": George Leighton and Richard Hellman," "Half Slave,

Half Free: Unemployment, the Depression and American Young People," *Harper's* magazine, August 1935, pp. 342–353.

12    "confused, disillusioned": Davis op. cit., p. 21.

12    "Top Ten School Problems": Mike Males, *The Scapegoat Generation,* Common Courage Press, 1996, p. 259.

12    the "slack" and the "doomed generation": Allan Mayer, "The Graying of America," *Newsweek,* February 28, 1977, p. 50.

13    was "not much": CBS News poll, October 9, 1979.

13    the Dartmouth valedictorian: William Strauss and Neil Howe, *Generations,* William Morrow and Co., 1991, p. 311.

13    "waiting for life": Ibid.

13    "The rising world shall sing": Ibid., p. 172.

14    "the twentysomething generation is balking": David M. Gross and Sophfronia Scott, "Proceeding with Caution," *Time,* July 16, 1990, pp. 56–62.

15    "where to point the camera": Clay Chandler, "Leave It to Beavis," *Washington Post,* February 18, 1996.

16    "during the falling apart": Jon Meacham, "Where Have All the Causes Gone," *Newsweek,* January 22, 1997.

16    "We are making our history every day": Letters, *Newsweek,* February 17, 1997.

16    "Gen X is committed": Margaret Homblower, "Great X-pectations," *Time,* June 9, 1997, pp. 58–68.

16    "the generation labeled X": Letters, *Time,* June 23, 1997.

17    70 million: U.S. Census figures, 1990.

18    "Fun events, fun logos, fun things": Jeff Shesol, "Fun in Politics? As If," *Washington Post,* March 2, 1997.

18    "I saw Hank lying on the ground": Bob Herbert, "Kids Know the Real Deal," *New York Times,* February 6, 1994.

21    60 percent of young people did not identify with either: The Polling Company, Luntz Research national surveys, 1996.

21    10 percent of twenty-five- to thirty-four-year-olds are starting their own businesses: Randall Lane, "Computers Are Our Friends," *Forbes,* May 8, 1995, pp. 102–108.

22    "I just put out colors I dig": Gregory Beals and Leslie Kaufman, "The Kids Know Cool," *Newsweek,* March 31, 1997, pp. 48–49.

22    In 1980, only 56 percent of children lived with two once-married parents: National Center for Health Statistics, *Supplements to the Monthly Vital Health Statistics Report* (series 24, no. 1), May 1989.

*Notes*

22    Four-fifths of their parents professed to be happier after their divorces: Marie Winn, *Children Without Childhood,* Pantheon, 1983, p. 139.

## Chapter One: Party Out of Bounds

28    Third Millennium to be the '90s equivalent of the 1962 Port Huron Statement: Cox News Service, July 15, 1993.

33    "valiant spokesmen": Stuart Miller, "The Death of Lead or Leave," *Swing,* November 1995, pp. 56–61.

34    "foot soldiers for democracy": Jonathan S. Cohn, "A Lost Political Generation?" *American Prospect,* no. 9, spring 1992, pp. 30–38.

34    voting percentage for 18–35s steadily dropped: Exit Poll Data, 1972–1996, Congressional Research Service Special Report.

34    "most boomers didn't even do . . . sex": Christopher Hitchins, "The Baby-Boomer Wasteland," *Vanity Fair,* January 1996, pp. 32–35.

35    "our generation's Vietnam": Andrew Cohen, "Twentysomething Stories: Me and My Zeitgeist," *The Nation,* July 19, 1993, pp. 96–100.

35    "Bobby Kennedy was my hero": Miller, op. cit., pp. 56–61.

35    "like talking politics with Marky Mark": Martin Kihn, "The Gen X Hucksters," *New York,* August 29, 1994, pp. 94–107.

36    a "million-member grass-roots organization": Jon Cowan and Rob Nelson, *Revolution X,* Penguin Books, 1994.

37    they listed their top concerns as: the economy, crime, education, and environment: Youth Vote '96 and Global Strategy Research national polls, 1996.

37    they listed "nothing" as their top concern: CBS News Issues Poll, October 9, 1979.

37    "a Gen-X PAC": Kihn, op. cit., pp. 94–107.

38    "[Their] future seems to lie in words": Michael Grunwald, "Making Their X," *Boston Globe Magazine,* November 29, 1993.

45    "galaxy and salvation army": William Strauss and Neil Howe, *Generations,* William Morrow and Co., 1991, p. 233.

46    "What we are seeing here": Stephen E. Ambrose, *Nixon: Triumph of a Politician, 1962–1972,* Simon & Schuster, 1989, p. 190.

46    "Richard Nixon Is a Closet Queen": Abbie Hoffman, Jerry Rubin, and Ed Sanders, *Vote!* Warner Books, 1972, p. 161.

46    "Nixon was uptight about the youth vote": Theodore E. White, *The Making of the President 1972,* p. 321.

46    More than 125,000 volunteers: "Youth Vote: Drives By All Sides to Get It to the Polls," *CQ Political Report,* August 5, 1972.

46 "Nixonettes": Hoffman et al, p. 156.

47 Nixon received about 57 percent: Exit Poll Data, 1972–1996, Congressional Research Service Special Report.

47 "young voters [are] the linchpin": *Washington Post,* September 15, 1992.

51 "The much ballyhooed 'Gen X' crowd": *O'Dwyer's Washington Report,* vol. 5, no. 2, January 17, 1995.

## Chapter Two: Open Commitment

55 young Hill staffers (average age, twenty-six): "Employment and Trends," U.S. Office of Personnel Management, 1996.

57 "Young Conservative Chic": Jamie Stiehm, *The Hill,* January 1995.

58 "Everybody knows MTV": Jon Shenk, *Who Cares* magazine, fall 1996.

58 40 percent of them had voted for Clinton: Exit Poll Data, 1972–1996, CRS Special Report.

59 Over 70 percent of registered Democrats in the primaries: Hamilton & Staff statewide poll, 1995.

60 over 50 percent of voters were registered as independents: Massachusetts Secretary of State's Office, 1996.

60 Thirty-seven percent of 18–35s considered themselves conservatives: The Polling Company national poll, 1996.

61 By the beginning of 1996: *Link* magazine survey, 1996.

62 40 percent of the 12 million new voters: Global Strategy Group Inc. Poll, 1996.

67 This was a bargain for the elderly: Neil Howe and Bill Strauss, "Rx for Generation X," *Washington Post,* June 13, 1994.

67 When New York State passed it in 1993: M. L. Mitchell and Richard Thau, "Don't Hand the Young the Health Bill," *New York Times,* July 24, 1994.

68 which claimed the plan would cost $59 billion: White House Estimate of Clinton Proposal, February 1994.

68 which said $74 billion: Analysis of Administration's Health Care Proposal, Congressional Budget Office, February 1994.

68 "I think most healthy, single Americans": "Clinton: Young, Single, Healthy to Pay Higher Premiums," *CongressDaily/National Journal,* September 16, 1993, p. 2.

68 "Medicare would only cost $9 billion": Original Medicare Cost Estimates, Congressional Research Service Report for Congress, Congressional Budget Office numbers.

71 over 40 percent of their grandparents: U.S. Census Bureau, 1996.

72 all of the national budget would be spent on the elderly: "The Federal Debt: Who Bears Its Burdens?" Congressional Research Service Issue Brief, March 1, 1996.

76 approximately 21 percent of the total vote: *New York Times* exit polls, 1996.

78 More than 50 percent of twelve- to seventeen-year-olds consider themselves independent: The Polling Company national poll, 1996.

80 The hospital trust fund, which was part of Medicare, was out of money: Treasury Department Report, 1995.

82 "My best judgment": Alison Mitchell, "President offers to back congressional effort to reduce costs of Medicare," *New York Times*, July 23, 1997.

## Chapter Three: Block by Block

85 "American priorities have shifted away": Mike Males, *Scapegoat Generation*, Common Courage Press, 1996, p. 15.

87 72 percent of students said they had performed: UCLA Higher Education Research College Freshman Survey, 1997.

89 "youngsters who . . . show us the blank, unremorseful stare": John DiIulio, "Stop Crime Where It Starts," *New York Times*, July 31, 1996.

89 700 pieces of legislation: Brent Staples, "The Littlest Killers," *New York Times*, February 6, 1995.

89 "These little turkeys": "Outloud," *U.S. News & World Report*, February 5, 1996.

90 84 percent of the nation's counties: Bureau of Criminal Justice Statistics, 1997.

90 House of Representatives . . . would vote to offer states $1.5 billion: U.S. House of Representatives, 1997.

90 the fifteen-year-old girl in Ohio who ran away from home: Anthony Lewis, "Suffer the Children," *New York Times*, July 1997.

92 "It's time for a new generation": Doug Struck, "Brash 12-Year-Old Overstepped Bounds," *Washington Post*, April 1997.

92 "I guess [he] wanted to die": Ibid.

92 preventive measures to be more cost-effective: RAND Corporation Study, 1996.

93 Over 74 percent of 18–35s believe: Global Strategy Research national poll, 1996.

93 make a genuine difference: Lake Research, Youth Voices '96 Poll.

94 "The only way to get out is to die": Perspectives, *Newsweek*, September 19, 1994.

94  "I am very . . ." "Sick": Nancy R. Gibbs, "Murder in Miniature," *Time*, September 19, 1994, pp. 55–59.

96  one in six kids between ten and seventeen had seen or knew someone who had been shot: *Newsweek*/Children's Defense Fund Poll, 1994.

96  children were 244 percent more likely to be killed by guns now than they were in 1986: FBI Uniform Crime Reports, 1994.

97  "never had a bond issue that was voted down": E. L. Boyer, *The Carnegie Foundation for the Advancement of Teaching High School: A Report on Secondary Education in America*, 1983, p. 19.

97  two-thirds of Americans were willing to pay extra taxes for schools: Ibid.

97  30 percent of Americans said they were willing to pay: Gallup Poll of Public's Attitudes Toward the Public Schools, 1981.

98  an estimated $25 billion in repairs: Boyer, op. cit.

98  "For the first time in the history of our country": National Commission on Excellence in Education Report, *A Nation At Risk* (1983), p. 42.

101  "The disappearance of the principle behind volunteering": Letters, *New York Times*, April 24, 1997.

101  "As graduation neared, a school official pulled me aside": Lynn Steirer, "When Volunteerism Isn't Noble," *New York Times*, April 22, 1997.

103  36 percent of kids today fixed their own meals: Yankelovich Youth Monitor, 1993.

103  In some classrooms nationwide: "Overdrive," *Time*, July 18, 1994.

### Chapter Four: The Selling of the Press-ident

108  "Think of an aging musician": Jeff Greenfield, *Time*, August 19, 1996.

111  the combined three-network audience fell 25 percent: Nielsen ratings.

113  "Young people can look at TV commercials": Sue Ellen Christian, "Youth Vote Is Nobody's Sure Thing," *Chicago Tribune*, June 10, 1996.

117  "I can't afford to make pop generalities": Martin Kihn, "The Gen X Hucksters, *New York*, August 19, 1994, pp. 94–107.

118  had become his least stable: Luntz Research national poll, 1994.

119  "[MTV] shouldn't feel the pressure": Manny Howard, "MTV Changes the Way Politics Was Covered," *George* magazine, June 1996.

119  "Here's our little pipsqueaks!": Tad Friend, "It's, Like, About Politics and Stuff," *New York Times Magazine*, June 15, 1997.

125  As network ratings fell from 43.2 percent: Roper Center Survey, March 1997.

125  85 percent of 18–35s watched *local* television news: Pew Research Center.

126 "Unfortunately, many watch little": Editorial, "Yo, Kids," *Los Angeles Times*, June 19, 1992.

127 "By spring '96": Jon Katz, "Birth of a Digital Nation," *Wired*, April 1997, p. 51.

127 most people tend to believe: *InfoWorld*, June 12, 1996.

128 homicide by youths under seventeen tripled: U.S. Department of Justice: Office of Juvenile Justice and Delinquency Prevention, 1996.

128 "The disease is adolescence": D. Foster, *Rolling Stone*, December 9, 1993, p. 55.

128 "Teen Crime Bomb": *U.S. News and World Report*, March 25, 1996, p. 28.

128 fifty-year-old men, murdered twice as many: FBI Uniform Crime Reports for the United States (1003).

128 The drug death rate among the peers of *Rolling Stone* publisher Jann Wenner: Substance Abuse & Mental Health Services Administration, 1995, and *Annual Medical Examiner Data*, 1993.

128 The record number of . . . deadbeat dads: K. M. Harris and F. F. Furstenberg Jr., "Divorce, Fathers and Children: Patterns and Effects of Paternal Involvement," presented at Population Association of America annual conference, April 7, 1995.

130 the average starting salary was $22,000: Library of Congress Report to Congress, Congressional Membership Office Operations, 1993.

131 "re-create the relaxed feeling": Friend, op. cit.

132 "There's something incredibly titillating": Ibid.

132 the Food Channel had a larger audience: Nielsen Ratings, July 1997.

## Chapter Five: Cyberpol Values

135 "a two-year-old start-up company": Steven Levy, "The Browser War," *Newsweek*, April 29, 1996.

135 Only 6.3 percent thought that "family values" was the most important: Global Strategy Research national poll, 1996.

138 "When Al Gore does it, the donor can't say that": *Time*, March 17, 1997.

138 "Silence from the Republicans": William Safire, "Saving Facepowder," *New York Times*, July 27, 1997.

143 After Ted Kennedy's Web site debuted: "How the Polls Are Spinning Webs," *National Journal*, December 9, 1995.

144 10 to 12 percent of voters had used the political Web sites: Pew Research Center, 1996.

145 40 percent of 18–35s, the highest of any age group: Baruch-Harris National Survey, 1996.

145 The average Internet user is a twenty-seven-year-old: Public Electronic Network study, *The Public Perspective*, June/July 1996.

146 42 departments and agencies within the federal government: General Accounting Office Report, 1997.

150 "Be prepared": *Christian America* Web site, November 1996.

151 Over 50 percent of adults offered negative descriptions of children: Public Agenda Report, *Kids These Days: What Americans Really Think About the Next Generation*, 1997, p. 11.

151 How likely they thought it was that they would be attacked by juveniles: RAND Corporation national poll, 1996.

151 "We had some activity a while back": Hanna Rosin, "Tupac is Everywhere," *New York*, June 2, 1997.

152 Children are techno-savvy and well-equipped: Jon Katz, "The Rights of Kids," *Wired*, July 1996.

153 "One of the functions of parents is monitoring": *InfoWorld*, June 12, 1996.

153 "Respect for elders": Public Agenda Report, op. cit., p. 11.

156 "farm team": *New York Times*, April 24, 1997.

156 "He will be able to earn fabulous sums": Ibid.

158 "threatens to torch a large segment": Supreme Court decision, *Reno v. American Civil Liberties Union*, June 26, 1997.

## Chapter Six: Year of the Woman

In addition to the following sources, the December 1995 report, *Do Women Vote for Women?*, distributed by the National Women's Political Caucus, and *Women on the Hill* by Clare Bingham (Times Books, 1997) were invaluable.

161 "In politics, women . . . type the letters": *Saturday Review*, September 15, 1974.

161 "This is unnatural": Meg Greenfield, "The Voters Look Away," *Washington Post*, October 13, 1996.

164 84 percent of 18–35s had answered yes: Luntz Research Poll, Global Strategy Research national poll, 1996.

165 "biggest coup in years": Jean F. Blashfield, *Hellraisers, Heroines and Holy Women*, St. Martin's Press, 1981, p. 55.

165 "if a young girl happens to be intelligent": Agnes E. Meyer, "Leadership Responsibilities of American Women," in *American Women: The Changing Image*, Beacon Press, 1962, p. 16.

165 "As far as I can judge": E. Erikson, *The Women in America*, Houghton Mifflin, 1965.

165 "If the party backs a woman": Peggy Lamson, *Few Are Chosen: American Women in Political Life Today*, Houghton Mifflin, 1968, p. xxiii.

169 "I recall a legislator from the Midwest": Sheila Tobias, *Faces of Feminism*, Westview, 1997.

170 "Pure in spirit": William Chafe, *The Paradox of Change: American Women in the 20th Century*, Oxford University Press, 1991, p. 25.

171 "There has to be respect": Pippa Norris, *Women, Media & Politics*, Oxford University Press, 1997.

172 "*Redbook* strategy": Christina Hoff Sommers, "The Democrats Secret Woman Weapon," *Washington Post*, January 5, 1997.

172 "For the time being": Ibid.

172 "no-risk feminism for a fearful age": Megan Rosenfeld, "Feminist Fatales," *Washington Post*, 1996.

173 "Say thank you": "Feminism's Daughters," Joannie M. Schrof, *U.S. News & World Report*, September 27, 1993, p. 20.

174 the proportion of mothers with children five and under who worked: "Family Crisis," *National Journal*, April 16, 1988.

174 women were overrepresented in clerical jobs in the House by 15 percent: Congressional Management Foundation, 1996 House and Senate Staff Employment: Salary, Trends, Demographics and Benefits.

178 "In plain language": E. J. Dionne, "One Big Mess, In Search of a Big Idea," *Washington Post*, July 27, 1997.

181 "We made a mistake": "Wal-Mart Apologizes for Dropping T-shirt," *Los Angeles Times*, September 24, 1995, p. 22.

181 "We have to urge them": Don Oldenburg, "The President Within," *Washington Post*, January 20, 1997.

182 women not only outnumbered men in graduate school: D. Furchtgott-Roth, C. Stolba, "Women's Figures: The Economic Progress of Women in America," Independent Women's Forum, 1996.

182 firms owned by women: Ibid.

## Chapter Seven: Party On

188 "I don't hate students": Associated Press, "Colleges No New Problem," *Bismark Tribune*, December 16, 1996, p. 1.

189 "Recent voter registration": Letter from Westy Byrd to Benjamin Wilson, October 23, 1996.

189  "It has long been established": Letter from Benjamin Wilson to Westy Byrd, October 25, 1996.

189  "If you have any legal authority": Letter from Westy Byrd to Benjamin Wilson, November 3, 1996.

196  "The confidence grew": E. J. Dionne, "One Big Mess, In Search of Big Ideas," *Washington Post*, July 27, 1997.

196  "Some believed that they were especially anointed": Ibid.

196  "The revolutionaries thought": Ibid.

200  "to darken our skies with toxic chemicals": Jon Cowan and Rob Nelson, *Revolution X*, Penguin Books, 1994, p. 180.

201  "It is incumbent on every generation": Letter from Thomas Jefferson to Destult de Tracy, 1820.

# Index